VOLUME 14   NUMBER 1   APRIL 2005

TRANSNATIONAL CORPORATIONS

United Nations
New York and Geneva, 2005
United Nations Conference on Trade and Development
Division on Investment, Technology and Enterprise Development

Editorial statement

Transnational Corporations (formerly *The CTC Reporter*) is a refereed journal published three times a year by UNCTAD. In the past, the Programme on Transnational Corporations was carried out by the United Nations Centre on Transnational Corporations (1975-1992) and by the Transnational Corporations and Management Division of the United Nations Department of Economic and Social Development (1992-1993). The basic objective of this journal is to publish articles and research notes that provide insights into the economic, legal, social and cultural impacts of transnational corporations in an increasingly global economy and the policy implications that arise therefrom. It focuses especially on political and economic issues related to transnational corporations. In addition, *Transnational Corporations* features book reviews. The journal welcomes contributions from the academic community, policy makers and staff members of research institutions and international organizations. Guidelines for contributors are given at the end of this issue.

Editor: Karl P. Sauvant
Deputy editor: Michael Lim
Associate editor: Grazia Ietto-Gillies
Book review editor: Shin Ohinata
Production manager: Tess Sabico
home page: http://www.unctad.org/TNC

Subscriptions

A subscription to *Transnational Corporations* for one year is US$ 45 (single issues are US$ 20). See p. 187 for details of how to subscribe, or contact any distributor of United Nations publications. United Nations, Sales Section, Room DC2-853, 2 UN Plaza, New York, NY 10017, United States – tel.: 1 212 963 3552; fax: 1 212 963 3062; e-mail: publications@un.org; or Palais des Nations, 1211 Geneva 10, Switzerland – tel.: 41 22 917 1234; fax: 41 22 917 0123; e-mail: unpubli@unog.ch.

Note

The opinions expressed in this publication are those of the authors and do not necessarily reflect the views of the United Nations. The term "country" as used in this journal also refers, as appropriate, to territories or areas; the designations employed and the presentation of the material do not imply the expression of any opinion whatsoever on the part of the Secretariat of the United Nations concerning the legal status of any country, territory, city or area or of its authorities, or concerning the delimitation of its frontiers or boundaries. In addition, the designations of country groups are intended solely for statistical or analytical convenience and do not necessarily express a judgement about the stage of development reached by a particular country or area in the development process.

Unless stated otherwise, all references to dollars ($) are to United States dollars.

iii

Acknowledgement

The editors of *Transnational Corporations* would like to thank the following persons for reviewing manuscripts from January through December 2004.

Olumuyiwa Alaba
Abbas J. Ali
Thomas Andersson
Bernadette Andreosso-O'Callaghan
Lucas Assuncao
Vasily Astrov
Prema-Chandra Athukorala
Olufemi Babarinde
V.N. Balasubramanyam
Frank Barry
Christian Bellak
Julian Birkinshaw
Magnus Blömstrom
John Cantwell
Francisco Castro
Catherine Co
Neil Coe
Peter Dicken
Nigel Driffield
John H. Dunning
Juan José Durán
Michael J. Enright
Carolyn Fischer
Torbjorn Fredriksson
Nick Freeman
Xiaolan Fu
Oleg Gavriliuck
Jens Gammelgaard
Michael Gestrin
Pervez Ghauri
Stephen S. Golub
Edward M. Graham
Robert Grosse
Michael W. Hansen
Chai Kah Hin
Locknie Hsu
Simona Iammarino
Rolf Jungnickel
Anna Krohwinkel-Karlsson
Ari Kokko
Ian Laird
Robert E. Lipsey
Kari Liuhto
Henry Loewendahl

Andrés Lopez
Sarianna M. Lundan
Colombo Massimo
Dermot McAleese
Charles Albert Michalet
Axel Michaelowa
Hafiz Mirza
Theodore H. Moran
Michael Mortimore
Lilach Nachum
Rajneesh Narula
Premila Nazareth
Peter Nunnenkamp
Sheila Page
Nicolas Perdikis
Nicholas Phelps
Carlo Pietrobelli
Michael Plummer
Aseem Prakash
Ravi Ramamurti
Eric Ramstetter
Rajah Rasiah
Patrick Robinson
Winfried Ruigrok
Reg Rumny
Albert Edward Safarian
Magdolna Sass
Kalpana Seethepalli
Xiaofang Shen
Oded Shenkar
Satwinder Singh
Elizabeth Smythe
John M. Stopford
Dirk Willem te Velde
Daniel Van Den Bulcke
Kenneth Vander Velde
Brendan Vickers
N.T. Wang
Todd Weiler
Christopher Wilkie
Alvin Wint
Shuje Yao
Henry Yeung
Alena Zemplinerová

Transnational Corporations

Volume 14, Number 1, April 2005

Contents

Exploring the relationship between FDI flows and CDM potential

Anne Arquit Niederberger and Raymond Saner[*]

Since it was conceived in 1997, the Clean Development Mechanism (CDM) has become much more concrete, and expectations and reality are beginning to confront one another in the emerging carbon marketplace. This article provides an overview of this innovative policy instrument, which is an element of the United Nations Kyoto Protocol, and questions the simplistic assumption that CDM flows will essentially mimic foreign direct investment (FDI) flows. By shedding light on the nature of the CDM and exploring the relationship between the CDM and investment, this article clarifies CDM-related determinants of FDI flows, suggests CDM opportunities for transnational corporations (TNCs) and outlines further research needed to determine how developing country entities can attract CDM investment or enhance their ability to export CDM certificates.

Introduction

Political overview of the UNFCCC and the Kyoto Protocol

The United Nations Framework Convention on Climate Change (UNFCCC) entered into force on 21 March 1994 and, by February 2005, had been ratified by 188 countries and the European Union. Delegates to the first session of the Conference of the Parties (COP1, Berlin, 1995) agreed that the commitments contained in the Convention for developed countries – to adopt

[*] Anne Arquit Niederberger (corresponding author) is an independent consultant at Policy Solutions, Hoboken NJ, United States (policy@optonline.net); Raymond Saner is Director of the Centre for Socio-Eco-Nomic Development in Geneva, Switzerland (saner@csend.org). The authors thank Karl P. Sauvant for encouraging them to prepare a manuscript on this topic, the anonymous peer reviewers and Martina Jung for their precise and constructive comments and the staff at CSEND for their research support.

policies and measures aimed at returning their greenhouse gas emissions to 1990 levels by the year 2000 – were inadequate to achieve its ultimate objective.[1] Therefore, they launched negotiations under the "Berlin Mandate" to define additional commitments. These negotiations continued at COP2 (Geneva, 1996) and culminated at COP3 (Kyoto, 1997) with the adoption of the Kyoto Protocol.

The Kyoto Protocol contains legally binding emissions targets for industrialized countries listed in Annex I of the agreement; these so-called "Annex I countries" are to reduce their collective emissions of six key greenhouse gases by at least 5% on average over the period 2008 – 2012, compared with 1990 levels.[2] This group target will be achieved through cuts of 8% by the European Union (EU) (the EU will meet its group target by distributing different rates among its members), most Central and Eastern European countries, and Switzerland; 7% by the United States; and 6% by Canada, Hungary, Japan and Poland. Russia, New Zealand and Ukraine are to stabilize their emissions, while Norway may increase emissions by up to 1%, Australia by up to 8% and Iceland 10%. The six gases are to be combined in a "basket", with reductions in individual gases translated into "CO_2 equivalents" that are then added up to produce a single figure.

The Marrakech Accords, adopted by the 7th session of the COP in 2001, paved the way for the ratification of the Protocol,

---

[1] The ultimate objective of the UNFCCC is the "stabilization of greenhouse gas concentrations in the atmosphere at a level that would prevent dangerous anthropogenic interference with the climate system. Such a level should be achieved within a time-frame sufficient to allow ecosystems to adapt naturally to climate change, to ensure that food production is not threatened and to enable economic development to proceed in a sustainable manner". The full text of the Convention is available at http://unfcc.int/essential background/convention/ background/items/2853.php.

[2] Cuts in the three most important gases – carbon dioxide (CO_2), methane (CH_4), nitrous oxide (N_2O) – will be measured against a base year of 1990 (with exceptions for some countries with economies in transition). Cuts in three groups of long-lived industrial gases – hydrofluorocarbons (HFCs), perfluorocarbons (PFCs), sulphur hexafluoride (SF_6) – can be measured against either a 1990 or 1995 baseline.

which entered into force on 16 February 2005. As of 11 April 2005, 148 governments and regional economic integration organizations had deposited instruments of ratification, with the United States – the largest single emitter of greenhouse gases, accounting for 36.1% of the 1990 carbon dioxide emissions of all Annex I countries combined – being prominent by its absence. The EU launched its own internal emissions trading system on 1 January 2005.

Background on the CDM

One of the novel features of the Kyoto regime is the inclusion of three so-called "Kyoto mechanisms", which give countries some flexibility in where, when and how they achieve the necessary greenhouse gas emission reductions. International emissions trading allows developed countries to buy and sell emission allowances among themselves. The project-based mechanisms – joint implementation and the Clean Development Mechanism (figure 1) – make it possible for developed countries to acquire fungible credits for greenhouse gas emission reductions that result from the implementation of climate protection projects in other Annex I or in non-Annex I countries, respectively, to which they contribute financially.

Figure 1. Schematic diagramme of the CDM

Climate change mitigation

Certified emission reductions

Local sustainable development

Source: Adapted from Arquit Niederberger and Albrecht, 1999.

The focus of this article is on the CDM, which has a twofold purpose, namely to assist:

- developing country (non-Annex I) parties in achieving sustainable development and contributing to the ultimate objective of the Convention; and
- developed country (Annex I) parties in achieving compliance with their emission limitation and reduction commitments under the Protocol.

Under the CDM, projects that result in real, measurable and long-term climate mitigation benefits (either reduced emissions of greenhouse gases or enhanced uptake/removal of carbon dioxide from the atmosphere), and which are additional to any emission reductions that would otherwise occur, can be validated as CDM projects. The range of sector and source categories that could be addressed via CDM project activities are indicated in table 1.

Table 1. Sectors/source categories for CDM

Greenhouse gas emission reductions			
Energy	Industrial processes	Agriculture	Waste
$CO_2 - CH_4 - N_2O$	$CO_2 - N_2O - HFCs - PFCs - SF_6$	$CH_4 - N_2O$	CH_4
Fuel combustion· • Energy industries· • Manufacturing industries· • Construction • Transport· • Other sectors Fugitive emissions from fuels· • Solid fuels· • Oil and natural gas	• Mineral products· • Chemical industry • Metal production • Production and consumption of halocarbons and sulphur hexafluoride • Solvent use • Others	• Enteric fermentation • Rice cultivation • Agricultural soils • Prescribed burning of savannas (cerrado) • Filed burning of agricultural residues • Others	• Solid waste disposal • Wastewater handling • Waste incineration· • Others
CO_2 removals			
Reforestation/afforestation			

Source: Lopez, 2002.

The actual emission reductions achieved by CDM projects are independently verified *ex post* and result in the issuance of certified emission reduction (CER) credits. These credits can be acquired by private and/or public entities and can be used to meet the Protocol obligations of developed countries. Each CER represents a reduction or sink enhancement equal to 1 ton of CO_2-equivalent emissions.

Recognizing that estimates for emerging markets are inherently uncertain, the potential market for the Kyoto mechanisms during the first commitment period (2008-2012) has been estimated to be in the range of hundreds of millions to tens of billions of dollars annually, with lower estimates resulting from the United States' rejection of the Kyoto Protocol (Springer, 2002; Springer and Varilek, 2004). The importance of the CDM in the overall carbon market will depend on a number of supply- and demand-side factors, for example, the strategy of the Russian Federation with respect to the management of its surplus emission allowances; the ability of non-Annex I countries to identify, develop and implement CDM projects; the efficacy of the CDM Executive Board (regarding approval of methodologies, project registration); the progress of Annex I countries in implementing domestic climate mitigation policies; and political decisions on the future evolution of the UNFCCC/ Kyoto regime beyond 2012 (Jotzo and Michaelowa, 2002; World Bank, 2004).

Generic CDM transaction types

The financial contribution of developed country entities (e.g. governments, private companies, market intermediaries) to CDM projects (or the international sourcing of CERs by them) can take a number of forms. The basic CDM transaction models from the perspective of Annex I (developed country) entities are:

•   Investments in CDM projects: equity investments (i.e. direct via joint venture companies/wholly owned subsidiaries, or indirect (portfolio) investments via the purchase of securities) that provide co-financing to projects that generate CER credits (investors receive the profit/return on investment[3] and CERs (see box 1 for examples)).

• Purchases of yet-to-be-generated CERs: forward contracts (e.g. in the form of a carbon purchase agreement) or call options to purchase a specified amount of CERs generated by a CDM project upon delivery, perhaps with some up-front payment.

• CER trades on secondary markets: spot or options transactions in existing CERs, generated either under the above models or unilaterally by project host country sources.

At present, the most common form of transaction is forward contracts to purchase CERs, which limits the risk to the buyer; Frank Lecocq (2004, p. 25) estimated the share of such "commodity transactions" in 2003-2004 at 95%. Recognizing that data on transaction types are notoriously hard to come by (because many deals are transacted confidentially), we have only been able to confirm two projects with approved baseline methodologies that involve FDI (box 1).

The share of CDM deals that each of the three CDM transaction models (i.e. investment in CDM projects, forward purchase of CERs, CER trades on secondary/spot markets) would represent in a mature market has not been analyzed in depth. Some observers have suggested that the volume of pure carbon purchase deals will be limited by underlying project financing challenges and that investment-type CDM deals involving private buyers might increase, now that the Kyoto Protocol has entered into force and companies have more clarity on their home country regulatory frameworks, a key driver of

---

[3] Return on investment is a measure of a corporation's profitability, equal to a fiscal year's income divided by stock equity plus long-term debt. It measures how effectively a firm uses its capital to generate profit.

demand. But others have pointed to the potential for unilateral CDM, which would lead to even more pure carbon purchase deals (Jahn *et al*., 2004).

Box 1. FDI in CDM projects

    The following CDM projects were among the first five for which baseline methodologies have been approved by the CDM Executive Board. They both involve equity FDI, which, in some cases, is directly linked to CER transfers:

- ***AT Biopower Rice Husk Power Project, Thailand***. Instead of the current practice (i.e. open-air burning or decay), this project will use rice husk to generate electricity, based on technology not yet used in Thailand. Rolls Royce Power Ventures (RRPV) holds a minority stake in AT Biopower. RRPV's investment is seen as a small contribution to the promotion of "green" projects and, although any sale of carbon credits would increase the expected return, RRPV believes that the project is robust enough to give a reasonable return without CDM cash flow. According to the baseline methodology and the project design document, CDM additionally is related to both financial (e.g. relatively low return on investment) and non-financial (e.g. perceived risk) investment barriers as well as the risk of introducing a new technology. The CERs are being contracted to Chubu Electric Power Company in Japan, which has its own voluntary target to reduce the carbon intensity of its electricity production (kg CO_2/kWh) by 20% between 1990-2010, and regards FDI linked to CDM as one means of achieving this target (Ito, 2004).

- ***Ulsan Chemical HFC 23 Decomposition Project, Republic of Korea***: INEOS Fluor Japan Ltd. has pioneered the application of technology for the decomposition of hydro fluorocarbons (HFCs) and other fluorocarbons produced by the fluorocarbon manufacturing process in its plants in Japan, the United

/...

Another important point to keep in mind when exploring the relationship between FDI and CDM flows is that – contrary to initial expectations – governments and hybrid entities (e.g. public-private partnerships, such as the funds offered by the World Bank's Carbon Finance practice) are significant players in the market. In 2003-2004, although Japanese private investors increased their market share to 41% (a doubling over 2002-2003), the World Bank Carbon Finance business (24%) and the Government of the Netherlands (23%) together still accounted for the largest share of the project-based emission reduction market in volume terms (Lecocq, 2004, p. 19). One analysis of the future importance of government vs. private sector buyers estimated that buyer governments will account for between about half and three-quarters of direct, international greenhouse gas compliance instrument purchases in 2010 (Natsource, 2003), but the trend over the past several years has been going in the opposite direction. In 2003, the private sector acting alone accounted for 45% of the total volume of emission reductions contracted in the developing world, double the share in 2002 (Lecocq and Capoor, 2003).

On the other hand, an increasing number of OECD country governments are developing and implementing public procurement programmes to purchase Kyoto certificates. Due to the rather generous allocations of emission allowances to the private sector under many of the National Allocation Plans under the EU Emission Trading Scheme (Gilbert, Bode and Phylipsen, 2004), EU governments will have to take up the slack to ensure compliance. How they choose to do this (i.e. policies that result in domestic reductions in non-regulated sectors vs. Kyoto mechanism transactions) will affect the balance of public vs. private sector demand for CERs, as well as the prevalence of FDI transactions. Some EU countries, such as the Netherlands, are actively engaging in CER procurement programmes that generally do not involve FDI.

With these two important observations in mind, the rest of this article considers the relationship between FDI and potential CDM flows. From the perspective of Annex I country entities, cross-border sourcing of greenhouse gas emission reductions can take two basic forms:
- arms-length trade (CER imports); and
- direct production of CERs through FDI (or other forms of equity investment) in CDM projects.

Under the prevailing CER forward purchase (trade) model, transactions will likely be governed by traditional factors of comparative advantages in production and trade, such as initial endowments (in particular, capital and labour), but low-cost greenhouse gas emission reduction and sink potentials will have to be added to the list of relevant initial endowments. The relationship between international trade flows and potential CDM flows is not the subject of this research note, but would warrant further consideration given the prevalence of CDM transactions in the form of CER trade. This article focuses instead on the direct production of CERs resulting from FDI by Annex I entities.

Analysis of FDI and CDM drivers and interactions

Overview of relevant FDI drivers and flows

For CDM transactions that do involve private equity investment, FDI flows might serve as a useful, albeit incomplete, indicator of potential CDM flows (Fankhauser and Lavric, 2003). UNCTAD defines FDI[4] as "an investment involving a long-term relationship and reflecting a lasting interest and control by a resident entity in one economy in an enterprise resident in an economy other than that of the foreign direct investor" (UNCTAD, 2003a, p. 31). More simply put, FDI involves direct investment in productive assets by a company established in a foreign country, as opposed to minority investment of less than 10% by foreign entities in local companies. Although a minimally enabling regulatory framework for FDI is a prerequisite for inward FDI, and business facilitation efforts can help to attract foreign direct investors, economic factors are the main determinant of FDI inflows and reflect the primary motivations of transnational corporations (see first two columns of table 2).

We suggest that the CDM might expand the traditional economic determinants of FDI, as TNCs perceive new CDM-related business opportunities (such as the production of CERs by foreign affiliates that also give them a competitive advantage (e.g. energy efficiency improvements)) and economic drivers (such as access to new markets for climate-friendly technologies or services). TNCs whose home countries are subject to emission limitations under the Kyoto Protocol, particularly those in sectors that are responsible for a significant share of greenhouse gas emissions, may be subject to domestic legislation to curb their emissions.

---

[4] FDI has three components: equity capital, reinvested earnings and intra-company loans or debt transactions (UNCTAD, 2003a, pp. 31-32). The extent to which each of these components might be linked to CDM transactions may have been considered by individual corporations with anticipated carbon liabilities, but has not been the subject of academic analysis to date.

Table 2. Traditional and potential CDM-related determinants of FDI inflows

Corporation motive	Traditional economic determinants	Additional CDM determinants	CDM relevance to TNCs
Market-seeking	• Per capita income • Market size • Market growth • Access to regional / global markets	• New/expanded markets in developing countries for: • climate friendly technologies • CDM-related services	• Technology providers • Providers of CDM-related services (e.g. consulting, brokerage, certification)
Resource/asset-seeking	• Access to labour • Access to raw materials • Adequate infrastructure	• Access to greenhouse gas reduction / sink enhancement opportunities (CERs) • Institutional prerequisites for host country CDM approval	• Emitters of greenhouse gases in regulated markets • Market intermediaries
Efficiency-seeking	• Differential comparative advantages • Better deployment of global resources	• Low-cost greenhouse gas reductions via CDM projects • Investment in foreign affiliate technology upgrades compensated with CERs	• Emitters of greenhouse gases in regulated markets • Corporations without home country greenhouse gas liabilities
Strategic asset-seeking	• Access to new competitive advantages	• Access to complementary CDM assets possessed by foreign-based firms, e.g.: • resources • project pipelines • expertise/capabilities • markets • Improved company valuation	• Providers of CDM-related services (e.g. consulting, brokerage, certification) • Market intermediaries • Corporations that own excess emission certificates obtained via CDM

Source: the authors, drawing for columns 1-3 from UNCTAD, 1998, p. 91, and Dunning and McKaig-Berliner, 2002, pp. 8-9.

The EU Emission Trading Scheme, for example, was launched at the beginning of 2005. It is a cap-and-trade system that will regulate the carbon dioxide emissions of over 12,000 facilities across the expanded EU (all 25 members) engaging in energy supply activities (even if the energy is for internal use) and/or the production of iron and steel; cement, glass, lime, brick and ceramics; or pulp and paper.[5] These companies/facilities will be allocated tradable emissions allowances each year. Companies whose emissions exceed their store of allowances will face hefty penalties (€40 per ton of excess carbon dioxide emitted annually during the period 2005-2007 and €100 per ton during the period 2008-2012) and will still be required to deliver the missing allowances. The first trade of EU allowances for compliance under the first commitment period of the Kyoto Protocol was transacted in early November 2004 at a price of 9 per ton of CO_2, and the 2005-07 vintages are currently trading at €7-8/ton CO_2. Thus the EU-Emission Trading Scheme provides an economic incentive for TNCs to consider lower-cost opportunities abroad, such as those under the CDM.

The Kyoto mechanisms also provide opportunities to technology providers to expand their market for state-of-the-art energy-efficient and climate-friendly technologies to developing countries, which, without CDM financing, may not be commercially viable in a developing country context. Yet business models that would involve the direct engagement of such companies in Kyoto-motivated FDI transactions (e.g. up-front capital investment, loans or rebates in exchange for CERs generated using company technologies) have not received much attention to date. An advanced technology company that plans to become carbon neutral, for example, might reap a double dividend from schemes to source greenhouse gas reductions from CDM projects that employ their own technologies.

---

[5] For details, see Directive 2003/87/EC of the European Parliament and of the Council of 13 October 2003 establishing a scheme for greenhouse gas emission allowance trading within the Community and amending Council Directive 96/61/EC. The Linking Directive is COM/2003/403.

Finally, TNCs that provide CDM-related services, such as legal services (advice on CDM contractual arrangements), CDM project validation and certification services, strategic consulting services (e.g. assessing potential CDM options/assets) or capacity building services have engaged in strategic asset-seeking FDI (merger and acquisition activity or strategic alliances) to gain new competetive advantages.

In addition to these direct economic determinants, CDM-related motivations for FDI transactions might also include maintaining a positive public image and foreign affiliates' licenses to operate in host countries by contributing to local sustainable development; gaining a better understanding of company carbon liabilities, in-house mitigation potential/costs and CDM benefits; gaining experience to be in a position to influence policy; and management of corporate social responsibility obligations and related risks.

The following section explores the extent to which these additional CDM drivers might lead TNCs to increase FDI and whether FDI flows can be expected to be a proxy for CDM flows. Despite decreasing global FDI flows since 2000, developing countries actually saw a rebound in inward FDI in 2003 (a 9% increase compared with 2002), a recovery further strengthened in 2004 (UNCTAD, 2004). Nonetheless, for 2002 and 2003, only a handful of CDM-eligible developing economies attracted FDI inflows of more than $2 billion annually, namely Bermuda, Brazil, Cayman Islands, China, Hong Kong (China), India, Republic of Korea, Malaysia, Mexico and Singapore (UNCTAD, 2004). Five of these are also the developing economies with the largest absolute greenhouse gas emissions: Brazil, China, India, Republic of Korea and Mexico (details are presented in table 3 and discussed below).

Mapping CDM potential against FDI flows

Sam Fankhauser and Lucia Lavric (2003) suggest that data on FDI flows per capita can serve as an indicator of relative investor satisfaction with the investment climate in different countries, and that the "business environment" is one of the three factors in determining the relative attractiveness of the joint implementation mechanism[6] for host countries that they investigated (the other two being the potential volume of low-cost greenhouse gas emission reductions or sink enhancement – which puts an upper bound on the scope for joint implementation/CDM – and the institutional capacity for Kyoto transactions (figure 2). Although our discussion of the situation in the top three emitting countries – China, India, Brazil – addresses each of these important dimensions, this section focuses on the business environment.

Figure 2. Key host country factors in joint implementation/ CDM transaction decisions

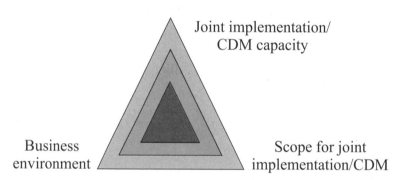

Source: the authors.

The response of investors to a poor business environment varies. Research has confirmed that foreign investors for the most part do not simply avoid countries without rule-based governance systems (Li, 2004) and with a high pervasiveness and arbitrariness of corruption (Doh *et al.*, 2003). Instead, they invest with different strategies: in poor governance environments, they tend to engage in FDI (rather than portfolio investment) or in the form of joint ventures with local partners,

---

[6] "Joint implementation" is another of the Kyoto mechanisms, similar to the CDM, but based on emission reduction projects hosted by industrialized, rather than developing, countries.

Table 3. Emissions and FDI data for potential CDM host countries

Economy	Population 2000 (Millions / % of world total)	Net GHG emissions 2000 (Mt CO$_2$)	Net emissions per capita ranking 2000	Inward FDI 2003 (dollar billion)	Inward FDI as a fraction of gross fixed capital formation, 2003 (%)	FDI performance index ranking 2001-2003[a]
China	1272 / 20.8	4899*	119	53.5	12.4	37
Hong Kong (China)	incl. above	incl. above	incl. above	13.6	38.4	9
India	1032 / 16.9	1797*	159	4.3	4.0[b]	114
Brazil	172 / 2.8	2215*	34	10.1	11.4	46
Mexico	99 / 1.6	609*	91	10.8	8.9	61
South Korea	47 / 0.8	528*	45	3.8	2.1	120

Sources: population, net greenhouse gas (GHG) emissions, emissions per capita: CAIT, 2005, available at: http://cait.wri.org; inward FDI 2003: UNCTAD, 2004, pp. 367-371; inward FDI as fraction of gross fixed capital formation: UNCTAD, 2004, pp. 387-398; FDI performance index: UNCTAD, 2004, p. 14).

a   The index is an ordinal ranking of 140 economies, with the rank of 1 representing the economy with the best performance.

b   Data for 2001.

*   These estimates do not necessarily correspond to official inventories that may have been prepared by the respective governments.

which provide them with greater management control and thus better protection. Yet there seems to be a threshold of corruption beyond which FDI becomes relatively unattractive. This applies to countries that exhibit both a high pervasiveness and arbitrariness of corruption. In such settings, entry modes that allow investors to transfer ownership (e.g. build-own-transfer or non-equity forms of FDI such as management contracts) are more attractive and prevalent than equity FDI (Doh *et al.*, 2003). This is consistent with the low ranking of such countries with respect to the UNCTAD Inward FDI Performance Index (UNCTAD, 2004, p. 14)). Given the large scope for low-cost greenhouse gas reductions and the prevalence of non-FDI entry modalities in these countries, FDI flows might not be a reliable indicator of potential Kyoto mechanism investment flows.[7]

Another challenge in considering the relationship between FDI flows and potential CDM flows is that FDI is defined at the level of enterprises, whereas the CDM is currently defined as a project-based activity. More research would be needed to determine under what conditions equity investment in foreign affiliates might be channeled into eligible CDM projects or why such FDI is, or is not, a good proxy for CDM project investment. In other words, investment in a company does not necessarily equate to an investment in eligible CDM project activities to mitigate climate change. This is particularly true for FDI that flows to the service sector, which tends to have a relatively low greenhouse gas intensity. In fact, an increasing share of FDI flows to the tertiary sector (which represented 55%-60% of FDI flows to developing countries from 1999-2001 (UNCTAD, 2003a, p. 192)), and may not correspond to the industries with the highest potential for CDM investment. Future research might compare the greenhouse gas reduction potentials of developing

---

[7] In an analysis of 13 economies in transition, an inverse relationship between the scope for joint implementation and the general business environment was found (Fankhauser and Lavric, 2003). Similar issues are being encountered by developing countries. As a result, host countries characterized by relatively low FDI attractiveness are turning to the unilateral CDM model to capitalize on their CDM potential (Jahn *et al.*, 2004).

countries by industry– taking into account project size and transaction costs – with their overall FDI performance and the distribution of inward FDI by sector.

The "big 3" developing countries from a greenhouse gas emissions perspective are China, India and Brazil (table 3), followed by the Republic of Korea and Mexico, all of which are significant FDI recipients. The FDI and CDM characteristics of China, India and Brazil are discussed below. According to a recent analysis of project-based pre-Kyoto compliance transactions (planned CDM and joint implementation projects), 36 host countries entered into such contracts in 2003, with nearly two-thirds of transacted volumes hosted by Latin American countries, approximately 30% by Asian countries (including 10 projects in India) and less than 5% by countries in sub-Saharan Africa (Lecocq and Capoor, 2003). The trend appears to be towards deals with large economies (e.g. India) or middle income countries (e.g. Brazil); the role of China is therefore expected to increase from its current low level.

FDI front-runner: China

Since 1991, China has been the largest non-OECD recipient of FDI inflows; in 2002, China garnered 10% of the world total ($52.7 billion), up from 3% in 1991 (UNCTAD, 2003a). China's success in attracting FDI can largely be attributed to traditional determinants of FDI, such as its large domestic market size, cost advantages and openness to the rest of the world (Dées, 1999). Interestingly – and of relevance to assessing whether FDI flows are a good predictor of future CDM investment flows – a large share of FDI in China during the 1990s was by non-resident Chinese based in Hong Kong (China), Taiwan Province of China and Singapore (Kumar, 1996, p. 9). These Chinese investors were mainly small and medium-sized enterprises which concentrated their investment in smaller, labour-intensive companies in eastern China. Consistent with this FDI focus, the sectoral emphasis of FDI was on manufacturing and services, with only 5% flowing to the energy sector[8] (IEA, 2003), even though at least half of China's CDM potential is anticipated in this sector (World Bank, 2004).

Central and western China lacked appeal to foreign investors because their industrial structures are predicated on resource-related industries, heavy and chemical industries as well as large enterprises, many of which were State owned (Jiang, 2001). But the geographical concentration of outdated, large-scale, State-owned industrial production in western, central and north-eastern China, coupled with increasing government regional development investments, social plans for laid off workers and incentives for these regions might signal CDM opportunities for TNCs, particularly in light of China's WTO membership. The liberalization of foreign investment policies and ongoing reforms in the energy industry are expected to help China to attract more foreign investment, particularly to help develop its western gas resources and in new electricity projects (IEA, 2003, p. 89).

China's CDM potential is uncertain, but expected to represent roughly half of total CDM supply during the first commitment period (World Bank, 2004). China is the second largest emitter of greenhouse gases worldwide. If unchecked, greenhouse gas emissions will grow rapidly in response to exploding energy demand in coming years. China's economy is still one of the most carbon-intensive worldwide, despite a remarkable decrease in its carbon intensity of nearly 50% between 1990 and 2000 (CAIT, 2005), so there is substantial potential for emission reductions (table 4 shows the source of emissions by sector).

Given market price expectations for the first commitment period of the Kyoto Protocol of less than \$10 per ton on a CO_2 equivalent basis, however, some of China's reduction potential will not be economical. The great bulk of inward FDI to China

---

[8] See Michaelowa *et al.*, 2003 for a succinct overview of FDI trends in the Chinese power industry.

Table 4. Greenhouse gas emissions, by sector, 2000, CO_2-equivalent basis

Country/sector	Million tons of carbon		Per cent	
China				
Energy	891.3		69.2	
Electricity & heat		*390.2*		*30.3*
Manufacturing & construction		*251.4*		*19.5*
Transportation		*59.8*		*4.6*
Other fuel combustion		*142.0*		*11.0*
Fugitive emissions[a]		*47.9*		*3.7*
Industrial processes[b]	101.9		7.9	
Agriculture	275.3		21.4	
Land-use change & forestry	-12.9		-1.0	
Waste	31.6		2.5	
Total	1 287.0			
India				
Energy	296.6		59.1	
Electricity & heat		*142.1*		*28.3*
Manufacturing & construction		*61.3*		*12.2*
Transportation		*34.3*		*6.8*
Other fuel combustion		*47.8*		*9.5*
Fugitive emissions[a]		*11.0*		*2.2*
Industrial processes[b]	17.8		3.6	
Agriculture	174.5		34.8	
Land-use change & forestry	-11.0		-2.2	
Waste	23.9		4.8	
Total	501.8			
Brazil				
Energy	87.6		14.5	
Electricity & heat		*10.4*		*1.7*
Manufacturing & construction		*25.7*		*4.3*
Transportation		*34.3*		*5.7*
Other fuel combustion		*14.9*		*2.5*
Fugitive emissions[a]		*2.3*		*0.4*
Industrial processes[b]	9.3		1.5	
Agriculture	121.7		20.2	
Land-use change & forestry	374.5		62.0	
Waste	10.9		1.8	
Total	604.1			

Source: CAIT, 2005.
[a] N_2O data not available.
[b] CH_4 data not available.
Note: 1 ton C = 3.6667 tons CO_2.

has flown into greenfield projects and, although the technology employed may not always represent the best available, it is often better than the economy-wide *status quo*. This means that marginal abatement costs in sectors with the greatest emission reduction potentials might be higher than anticipated.

In a recent study, China's CDM potential was judged to be distributed across the economy as follows: electricity generation, 50%; steel and cement production, 10% each; non-CO_2 projects (in particular, HFC-23 decomposition and methane capture), 10%; chemical industry, 5%; and other industries, 15% (World Bank, 2004). China's potential for carbon dioxide emission reductions related to energy supply and end-use during the first Kyoto Protocol commitment period (2008-2012) was estimated at between 25 and 117 million tons CO_2 annually[9] (World Bank, 2004).

Despite its documented CDM potential, China was slow to ensure the necessary institutional prerequisites and build a critical mass of CDM capacity. As a result, few potential CDM projects are currently in an advanced stage of development. Recently, however, the World Bank Prototype Carbon Fund announced that it will purchase 4.5 million CERs from a Chinese coalmine methane project over 20 years, and, since 2001, the Government has commissioned a number of CDM studies and launched capacity building efforts (World Bank, 2004).

As a result of a more proactive Government policy over the past year, a Designated National Authority was appointed and interim rules and procedures for domestic CDM approval went into effect on 30 June 2004, paving the way for Chinese

---

[9] This estimate of China's market share is broadly consistent with another recent independent analysis, which estimated China's technical potential for CDM activities related to energy supply and demand at about 350 million tons of CO_2 equivalent annually (Michaelowa *et al.*, 2003).

involvement in emerging carbon markets. Although the proactive position adopted by the Government is an encouraging sign, several provisions in the interim CDM regulation – such as the requirement for majority Chinese ownership of the local project participant and benefits sharing provisions – may discourage investors (Arquit Niederberger, 2004). The requirement that the local project partner be under Chinese control may also be problematic. In the power industry, for example, where FDI commonly takes the form of joint ventures with a local governmental organization, the foreign direct investor in three quarters of the joint ventures has a controlling interest (Michaelowa *et al.*, 2003), which would prohibit such entities from engaging in CDM project activities.

With China's substantial and growing market- and resource-seeking outward FDI, mainly driven by growing domestic competition and a need to access energy and other resources, Chinese TNCs could also profit from additional CER sales to Annex I entities associated with its own outward FDI projects in Asia or Africa. Similarly, non-Annex I economy TNCs investing in China, such as those from Hong Kong, China, could leverage additional CDM income streams from Annex I entities. Such CDM-related business opportunities for TNCs from developing economies investing in non-Annex I countries have scarcely been considered.

Overall, China has a significant CDM potential (energy efficiency, fuel switching, nitrous oxide, HFC-23 decomposition) and a recently improved institutional framework. It is rapidly gaining experience with real CDM projects. Experts regard China as an increasingly favourable country for CDM transactions, as evidenced by improved host country rankings (table 5).

Table 5. Point carbon CDM host country ratings, December 2004

Country	Rating	Interpretation	Rank
India	BBB	("somewhat attractive")	1
Chile	BBB	"	2
Brasil	BB	("not totally unattractive")	3
South Korea	BB	"	4
Peru	B	("slightly better than 50:50 chance that	5
China	B	CDM investments will succeed")	6
Morocco	B	"	7
Mexico	B	"	8

Source: Point Carbon, 2004.

Note: the rating of CDM host countries is based on Point Carbon's methodology, which includes an assessment of 14 indicators to evaluate host countries' institutional conditions for CDM, investment climate, as well as project status and potential. See http://www.pointcarbon.com/category.php?category ID=323&collapse=323 for further details.

FDI under-performer: India

Compared to China, India's inward FDI and FDI stock as a percentage of GDP are much lower. But expectations are that continued policy reforms will lead to greater inward FDI, even though other forms of partnerships (e.g. licensing, outsourcing) have proven to be efficient in areas of Indian specialization such as information technology services, call centers, business back-office operations, and research and development (UNCTAD, 2003a). According to the Confederation of Indian Industry, foreign investment has mainly been in the power, transport, chemicals, and paper industries, and investment has come primarily from countries that are now obligated under the Kyoto Protocol and domestic legislation to abate greenhouse gas emissions.[10] Since marginal abatement costs are generally lower in developing countries, additional

---

[10] See http://www.ciionline.org/services/78/default.asp?Page=CDM %20Projects.htm.

foreign investment and partnership is expected from these countries for climate change mitigation (e.g. technology cooperation, partial or full financing).

India has the second largest absolute greenhouse gas emissions of any potential CDM host country (table 3). Of the top three developing country emitters, it has by far the lowest emissions per capita (less than one ton of CO_2-equivalent per capita (GOI, 2004)). Given India's low level of income (less than $500 per capita) and access to energy services, coupled with its heavy reliance on coal, the country's emissions are expected to multiply rapidly without technological leapfrogging and policy measures. India's power demand alone is expected to increase by 3.5 times from 2000 to 2020 (Indian Planning Commission, 2002). The prevalence of inefficient technology and the need to provide energy services to a growing population means that opportunities for CDM investment could be substantial in the power generation (clean coal, renewables) and industrial (e.g. iron/steel, cement) sectors[11] (World Bank, forthcoming). India's CDM potential during the first commitment period of the Kyoto Protocol has been estimated at about 10% of the total CDM market (World Bank, forthcoming). The Confederation of Indian Industry estimates the mitigation opportunities in various industries as follows:[12]

- coal washing (reduce ash content from 40% to 30%): 11 million tons CO_2 equivalent annually;
- fuel switching (use imported liquified natural gas to replace coal-fired generation): four million tons CO_2 equivalent annually;

---

[11] It should be noted that, in addition to energy supply and end-use (which accounted for 61% of Indian greenhouse gas emissions in 1994), fully 29% of India's emissions were from agriculture, mainly enteric fermentation and rice paddy cultivation (GOI, 2004, p. 32). These official government figures are roughly consistent with the data provided in figure 3.

[12] The Conorederation also provides data on the total investment cost and the amount of electricity generation that the various options could encompass. For full information and data references, see http://www.ciionline.org/ services/78/default.asp?Page=Mitigation%20 Opportunities.htm.

- conventional efficiency (improve thermal efficiency 1.5%): four million tons CO_2 equivalent annually;
- integrated gas combined cycle power (install relevant technologies): five million tons CO_2 equivalent annually;
- renewables (wind, solar, bagasse, mini hydro): 60 million tons CO_2 equivalent annually.

In fact, India is emerging as a leader in CDM transactions in the nascent Kyoto pre-compliance market, with more CDM projects under development than any other host country (CDM Watch, 2004). About a quarter of all baseline and monitoring methodologies submitted for CDM Executive Board approval have come from Indian project developers. An important factor is the active role that Indian industry has taken. With support from USAID, for example, the Confederation of Indian Industry established a Climate Change Center to build awareness of climate change issues within Indian industry, promote consensus on the CDM, build local capacity to develop climate change mitigation projects, and to develop a pipeline of projects. Potential buyers have also funded project design document development (World Bank, forthcoming). Complementing the efforts of the private sector is the Indian National CDM Authority, which has already approved 25 projects. In a recent rating by Point Carbon (table 4), India was the top-ranked CDM host country.

FDI success in Brazil

Brazil has also been very successful in attracting FDI and – despite a 26% drop in FDI from the previous year to $16.6 billion in 2002 – it remains the largest recipient in Latin America. While the significance of FDI in the economy as measured by inflows as a percentage of gross fixed capital formation declined from 23% in 2001 to 20% in 2002, measured by FDI stock as a percentage of GDP it increased from 43% to 52% between 2001 and 2002.

TNCs from developed countries remain the largest investors in the Brazilian market, with the United States responsible for a quarter of FDI inflows over the 1990s. Since the current United States administration has said that it will not ratify the Kyoto Protocol, inward FDI from the United States may not be linked to significant interest in CDM investment. In 2002, however, the majority of the largest three foreign affiliates in all three sectors originated in Europe, in particular, the Netherlands, Spain and the United Kingdom (UNCTAD, 2003b):

* industrial sector: Japan (metals), Germany (motor vehicles), Netherlands/United Kingdom (petroleum);
* tertiary sector: Spain (telecom), France (trade), Netherlands (trade);
* finance: Netherlands, Spain, United Kingdom.

FDI stock in the primary sector declined sharply in 2002, while FDI in the secondary sector increased slightly, led by manufacturing in the food, automobile and chemicals industries (UNCTAD, 2003a, p. 54). FDI in the services sector declined from $1.6 billion in 2001 to $1.0 billion in 2002. In 1998, the three most important industries in terms of FDI stock were business activities (31%), finance (12%) and electricity, gas and water (8%), a major shift of emphasis since 1990.

In contrast to China and to a lesser extent India, Brazil's energy-related emissions are dwarfed by emissions from deforestation (over 60% of total emissions) and agriculture (table 5). Nonetheless, there is potential for CDM projects in energy (fuel substitution, energy efficiency) and industrial activities (process change, energy efficiency, fuel substitution), in particular, in basic materials industries such as aluminium, cement, chemicals, ferroalloys, iron and steel, pulp and paper (UNIDO, 2003), many of which currently attract FDI.[13]

---

[13] For further CDM/FDI information on the South American region see Morera, Cabeza and Black-Arbeláez, 2004.

Brazil was the first country to sign the United Nations Framework Convention on Climate Change and its proposal for a Clean Development Fund was the catalyst for international negotiations that culminated in the definition of the CDM contained in the Kyoto Protocol. The country was among the first to establish the required Designated National Authority to approve CDM projects, i.e. the Interministerial Committee for Global Climate Change (by Presidential Decree in July 1999). It is also engaged in a large number of CDM project identification and development activities by different promoters. Various institutions, such as UNCTAD and the World Business Council for Sustainable Development have supported CDM capacity building efforts as well.[14] The Brasilian Designated National Authority has already approved two CDM projects, with about 10 in the pipeline (Miguez, 2004). One of these – the Brazil NovaGerar Landfill Gas to Energy Project – is the first (and, to date, one of only two) CDM projects to have been officially registered by the CDM Executive Board on 18 November 2004.[15]

In general, Brazil is regarded by the international business community as one of the most attractive countries to host CDM projects (UNIDO, 2003). A number of TNCs are already involved in various types of CDM transactions there, although none involve FDI (box 2). Point Carbon ranked Brasil as the third most attractive host country for CDM projects (table 4).

---

[14] These activities were both part of the United Nations Foundation supported project "Engaging the Private Sector in the Clean Development Mechanism". For further information on the UNCTAD programme, see http://r0.unctad.org/ghg/sitecurrent/projects/engaging_psic.html, and for information on lessons learned from its Brasilian rural solar energy case study, undertaken in partnership with British Petroleum, UNDP and UNIDO, refer to WBCSD, 2004.

[15] See http://cdm.unfccc.int/Projects/DNV-CUK1095236970.6/view.html for futher details on this project.

Box 2. Involvement of TNCs in Brasilian CDM project development

BP/PRODEEM Solar Project. BP Amoco (in association with PRODEEM, a programme of the Brazilian Ministry of Mines and Energy aimed at providing sustainable energy to schools and community buildings in rural areas of the country) won a contract from the Government of Brazil to supply 1,852 rural schools in 12 states in North-Eastern Brazil with solar electricity. The total cost of solar panels and their installation was financed by the Federal Government; BP ensures maintenance and upkeep for three years. This project was undertaken in cooperation with the World Business Council for Sustainable Development to provide a working business example of a CDM project and to contribute to CDM rule-making and capacity building (see WBCSD, 2004, for further details). The project has been completed outside of the CDM (prior to the entry into force of the Kyoto Protocol).

Prototype Carbon Fund Plantar Project. The World Bank Prototype Carbon Fund will purchase certified emission reductions generated by this project, which involves the establishment of 23,100 hectares of high yielding Eucalyptus varieties to produce wood for charcoal production to displace coke produced from coal in pig iron production; the reduction of methane emissions during charcoal production; and the regeneration of native vegetation on 478.3 hectares of pasture land. Investors in the Prototype Carbon Fund include six governments and 17 private enterprises.

V&M do Brasil Avoided Fuel Switch Project. The International Finance Corporation "Netherlands Carbon Facility" will provide a conditional commitment to the Brazilian steel producer V&M do Brasil to purchase five million tonnes of greenhouse gas emission reductions resulting from the continued use of plantation-derived charcoal in the production of steel instead of switching to coke made from imported coal. The total contract value is expected to be €15 million. Toyota Tsusho Corporation will sign a contract with V&M to purchase an additional volume of emission reductions that the project will generate.

Source: based on WBCSD, 2004, http://carbonfinance.org/pcf/router.cfm?Page=ProjectsID=3109 and other materials.

TNCs, climate risks/opportunities and CDM

In order to assess whether it is reasonable to expect a link between FDI at the level of companies and project-level CDM flows, it is necessary to understand the potential motivation of TNCs that emit greenhouse gases and have a need for CDM offsets or see value in acquiring such offsets for resale.

The 20 largest TNCs in UNFCCC Annex II countries in terms of foreign assets are concentrated in the telecoms (e.g. Vodafone, Deutsche Telekom AG, Telefonica SA), petroleum (BP, Exxonmobil, Royal Dutch/Shell, TotalFinaElf, ChevronTexaco Corp) and automotive (Ford Motor Company, General Motors, Toyota, Fiat, Volkswagen, Honda) industries. The electrical and electronic equipment producer General Electric ranks second (UNCTAD, 2003a, p. 187). Companies in the petroleum industry have the largest potential carbon liabilities with respect to domestic climate policies in their home countries, as they are major sources of greenhouse gas emissions, and British Petroleum and Royal Dutch/Shell have been leaders in the development of carbon markets. It is likely that such companies will continue to seek out low-cost mitigation opportunities in their foreign affiliates that can contribute to compliance of the parent enterprise or foreign affiliates in regulated markets and to diversify their worldwide operations to less carbon-intensive energy sources. But it is difficult to predict what role the CDM will play in overall company strategies and to what extent any CDM engagement will be in the form of FDI. In addition to in-house reductions, BP Australia is marketing its carbon neutral BP Ultimate and autogas fuels under the greenhouse friendly label. But, according to the terms of the Australian programme, the carbon offsets must be obtained through mitigation projects in Australia.[16] A similar model that would involve investment in CDM projects is conceivable.

---

[16] For further information, see www.greenhouse.gov.au/greenhousefriendly/consumers/products.html.

The transport industry is responsible for as much as one third of greenhouse gas emissions of Annex II countries, and is therefore a logical target for direct (e.g. new car fuel efficiency standards) or indirect (e.g. carbon taxes on transport fuels) emission controls. Car makers exporting to regulated markets must therefore develop their product lines to respond to demand for lower emission vehicles. Climate change policy can thus offer business opportunities for low-emission vehicles; but, so far, only the introduction of fuel cell buses has been considered as a potential CDM project. On the other hand, some Japanese and European car makers are exploring CDM opportunities as a pure compliance instrument, because the production of cars causes direct greenhouse gas emissions that may be subject to regulation or taxation. The United States auto makers have the greatest carbon intensity of production (due, in part, to the fact that they are more vertically integrated). But since greenhouse gas emissions are not regulated in the United States and because United States car makers rely to a large extent on the domestic market, their direct and indirect exposure is somewhat buffered in the short-term (Innovest, 2001).

Since five of the world's largest TNCs are from the United States – which currently does not plan to ratify the Kyoto Protocol – so it is unclear whether they will be able to profit from investment in CDM-type transactions. Certainly, their foreign affiliates operating in regulated markets or in CDM host countries could have a business interest.

Preliminary insights

Relationship between FDI flows and CDM potential

From a global perspective, current trends in FDI flows give some indication of the preferences of foreign investors. One element in common with the CDM is the quality of the general business environment. However, for a number of reasons, FDI flows do not necessarily reflect CDM market potential:

- CDM demand comes from both governments and the private sector, which might have different motivations and preferences. And private sector demand for emission reductions is not all associated with TNCs that operate in developing markets.
- Conversely, not all TNCs have an interest in Kyoto compliance instruments such as CERs from CDM projects, and some might not have a compelling incentive to make the required additional investment in climate mitigation.
- CDM transactions are predominantly in the form of CER trade, rather than equity investment in CDM projects, and not all equity investment in CDM projects will be in the form of direct investment.
- FDI might flow to industries/economies that do not represent large CDM potential and *vice versa*. (India, for example, is expected to be a major supplier of CERs, but its inward FDI is low and non-equity FDI mainly flows to telecoms, information technology and business services, which do not have substantial CDM potential.)
- FDI flows to companies do not guarantee investments in climate change mitigation efforts that meet CDM criteria, although technologies that are transferred to developing countries in connection with FDI generally tend to be more modern and environmentally "cleaner" than what is locally available (OECD, 2002). Greenfield FDI may even increase absolute greenhouse gas emissions in a host country.
- The necessary institutional prerequisites, specialized capacity and incentives to facilitate CDM investments and keep transaction costs low might be lacking in potential CDM host countries.

These observations are reflected by the fact that the largest CDM-eligible emitters of greenhouse gases (with greenhouse gas emissions over 100 million tons of carbon annually[17]) –

---

[17] On a CO_2 equivalent basis. See Climate Analysis Indicators Tool (CAIT) Version 2.0 (Washington, DC: World Resources Institute, 2005), available at: http://cait.wri.org.

---

which are also believed to have significant CDM potential – are distributed across three of the four cells of the UNCTAD FDI matrix (table 6). In fact, with the exception of Brazil, China and Mexico, the developing countries with the largest emissions exhibit low FDI performance. And India – classified as an FDI under-performer with low FDI potential (UNCTAD, 2004) – hosts more potential CDM projects currently under development than any of the other 26 host countries (CDM Watch, 2004).

Table 6. Relationship of largest developing country greenhouse gas emitters (absolute basis) to UNCTAD FDI matrix, 2000-2002

	High FDI performance	Low FDI performance
High FDI potential	FDI front- runners Brazil (3), China (1)	Below potential Iran (7), South Africa (8)
Low FDI potential	Mexico (5) Above potential	Republic of Korea (4) FDI under-performers India (2), Indonesia (6)

Sources: UNCTAD, 2004, p. 17, CAIT, 2005.
Note: Numbers in brackets represent the ordinal rank of the country with respect to absolute emissions, with 1 being the greatest emissions, on a CO_2 equivalent basis.

Overall investment climate and CDM considerations

It is not obvious that the overall investment climate is a good proxy for the more specific CDM investment climate. Among FDI front-runners, a number of Latin American countries, such as Chile, Costa Rica and Mexico, have taken the initiative to promote CDM activities and have attracted a greater share of fledgling CDM transfers than the FDI giant China, which only recently established the necessary institutional prerequisites. The reason for this is that these Latin American countries have invested in the necessary domestic CDM capacity[18] (e.g. CDM awareness and training programmes,

---

[18] For an example of CDM capacity building in Latin America, see Saner, Jáuregui and Yiu, 2001.

analysis of CDM potential, facilitation of project identification) and are committed to efficient institutional arrangements to promote and process CDM projects, which keeps transaction costs low.

Furthermore, contractual arrangements can help minimize country risk associated with CDM deals, assuming that these are in the form of carbon purchase agreements. India, for example, which is an "FDI underachiever", has been the most active country in terms of submissions of projects for validation under the CDM. The projects have mostly been small-scale renewable projects, with the exception of some large, non-CO_2 projects. As mentioned earlier, unilateral CDM, implemented without the involvement of entities from a third party, is one way that countries with a poor investment climate are hoping to take advantage of the Kyoto mechanisms, although it remains unclear whether the CDM Executive Board will endorse this approach. Indian project developers recently submitted the first Project Design Document and proposed a new baseline methodology for a unilateral CDM project, which should lead to clarification on the issue by the Executive Board.

Implications of FDI flows for CDM additionality

If a large amount of FDI is going into a certain sector of a country, this implies that the risk-return relationship in that sector is favourable to foreign investors under prevailing global market and domestic regulatory conditions in the country. As mentioned above, evidence suggests that technologies that are transferred to developing countries in connection with FDI generally tend to be more modern and environmentally friendly than what is locally available, perhaps lowering the business-as-usual emissions baseline. It has been shown that a significant fraction of TNCs self-regulate environmental aspects of their activities (e.g. OECD Guidelines for Multinational Enterprises, International Finance Corporation (IFC) Equator Principles, company policies), which is perceived to have a strong positive influence on the environmental performance of foreign affiliates. In fact, 30% of Asian foreign affiliates of TNCs involved in a recent study claim that foreign affiliates operate according to home country standards (Hansen, 2003). Even the IFC – the private sector lending arm of the World Bank – has detected a "huge interest in sustainability issues, coupled with the demand for innovative solutions" (Woicke, 2004). The typically better environmental performance of foreign affiliates might make it more difficult to demonstrate the additionality of climate protection projects in sectors/enterprises that attract much FDI (although investment barriers are not the only ones conceivable), and it may be more expensive for TNCs to make additional CDM investments in their own plants. On the other hand, many companies have been surprised at the amount of no regret mitigation potential they have uncovered, resulting in substantial net savings to their bottom lines.

Ignored by FDI, courted by CDM?

In reviewing the literature on determinants of inward FDI at the national level, Nagesh Kumar (1996, pp. 8-9) concluded that low income, agrarian economies with relatively poor infrastructure have limited scope for attracting FDI inflows, regardless of whether their policies are trade-friendly (e.g. liberalization of trade policy regimes, investment incentives, protection of intellectual property rights). This conclusion is consistent with declining shares of low income countries in South Asia and sub-Saharan Africa in global FDI inflows, despite the liberalization of trade and investment regimes. FDI flows have remained very modest, compared with other regions, such as Asia and Latin America, and TNCs have not made as significant a contribution as elsewhere. According to the OECD (2003), FDI in these sub-regions has been largely limited to investments in petroleum and other natural resources, and the TNCs have focused their activities on areas where returns are high enough to offset perceived risks of investing. In such cases, it might be difficult to argue convincingly that modest additional CDM financing is required to make a project commercially viable, but it is still conceivable that the CDM could help to overcome non-financial barriers to implementing some climate mitigation projects.

The backbone of the African private sector at present, however, is micro, small and medium-scale enterprises that often operate in the informal economy, yet most trade and investment promotion institutions do not reach them and channels for financial intermediation are ill-adapted to their needs (OECD, 2003). Efforts to attract more diverse FDI projects must go hand in hand with developing clusters of enterprises and sub-contracting or vendor programmes to link better these enterprises to those operating in the modern economy. Similar efforts are needed to promote the development of carbon sequestration and small-scale rural energy supply or efficiency projects that are expected to be particularly important for CDM in many African countries. The World Bank's new Community Development Carbon Fund specifically targets small-scale projects in least developed countries and the poorer regions of other developing countries. To date, large hydropower and waste-to-energy projects that involve methane emission reductions have attracted the greatest CDM investor interest (CDM Watch, 2004).

Implications and need for further research

This article suggests that the simplistic assumption that CDM financial flows will be correlated closely with FDI flows may not hold and warrants further analysis. More importantly, however, further research is needed to determine how developing country entities can attract CDM investment or enhance their ability to export CERs. This will require a more detailed analysis of:

- the sources of demand (countries, government vs. private sector investors and investors' CDM preferences);
- the dynamics of evolving carbon markets;
- the different CDM transaction models (equity investment in CDM projects vs. *ex ante* CER purchase agreements vs. secondary market CER trades); and
- the national determinants of CDM financial flows.

The UNCTAD / Earth Council Institute Carbon Market Programme is one initiative to investigate these trade- and investment-related CDM issues.

Furthermore, the results reported in this article have important policy implications for the full spectrum of actors in the CDM and carbon markets. For example:

*   Countries that have not been successful at attracting classic equity FDI, such as India or Latin American countries, can still be successful CDM host countries, particularly under carbon purchase arrangements. However, the underlying project finance remains a challenge, and countries must act fast to ensure that the necessary institutional prerequisites are met, as the window of opportunity for the first commitment period under the Kyoto Protocol (2008-2012) is rapidly closing.
*   Conversely, even FDI front-runners like China will have to adopt a proactive and supportive institutional, regulatory and policy framework to capture CDM potentials.
*   TNCs can benefit in a variety of ways from the CDM. To date, some companies that anticipate greenhouse gas regulation in their home country have considered the CDM as a compliance tool, which may or may not be linked to FDI. The CDM may also open new strategic opportunities to technology providers, financial intermediaries or developing country TNCs operating in other CDM host countries, but these emerging opportunities have scarcely been explored. Host country companies that succeed in leveraging CDM finance for their investment projects might gain a competitive advantage.
*   Information on the drivers, financial structure and transaction type of emerging private sector CDM deals is generally confidential, but would help CDM host country policymakers and project developers to respond better to CDM demand (via targeted incentives, awareness-raising, capacity building and project identification).
*   The future price for CERs is highly uncertain. Low prices will limit the scope for the potential value added of CDM to influence investment choices, particularly with respect to large projects for which the additional CDM finance is a small fraction of the total and has little influence on the project's return on investment. Under these circumstances,

public-private partnerships that combine CDM funding with other incentives, such as host government support for priority demonstration projects, could be essential. Care must be taken, however, that the incentives offered do not run counter to WTO provisions (Assunção and Zhang, 2002).

TNCs should investigate their potential carbon liabilities and CDM opportunities to consider if and how they can take advantage of emerging carbon markets to enhance their bottom line, while contributing to the protection of the global climate system and the sustainable development of CDM host countries. The CDM will not offer the same incentives to all companies, but could be particularly attractive to companies operating in regulated markets, such as the EU, or which produce climate-friendly advanced technologies or have significant low-cost greenhouse gas reduction potential in their foreign affiliates. CDM host countries, in turn, should assess the linkages between trade, investment and environmental issues (OECD, 2001) and consider how they can leverage CDM financial flows in support of their development priorities. ∎

References

Arquit Niederberger, Anne (2004) "CDM in China: taking a proactive and sustainable approach", *Joint Implementation Quarterly,* 10(3), p. 5.

Arquit Niederberger, Anne and Christian Albrecht (1999) "Internationale Zusammenarbeit zum Klimaschutz: Chance für Wirtschaft", *Umwelt Focus,* 6, pp. 17-21.

Assunção, Lucas and Zhong Xiang Zhang (2002) "Domestic climate policies and the WTO", Downloaded from the UNCTAD web site (r0.unctad.org/ghg/sitecurrent/download_c/pdf/ WTO_and_domestic_climate_policies.pdf).

CAIT (2005). *Climate Analysis Indicators Tool, Version 2.0.* (Washington, DC: World Resources Institute), available at: http://cait.wri.org.

CDM Watch (2004). *Clean Development Mechanism Status Note – March 2004,* CDM Watch web site (www.cdmwatch.org/files/2004%20status%20note.pdf).

Dées, Stéphane (1999). "Foreign direct investment in China: determinants and effects", *Economics of Planning*, 31(2-3), pp. 175-194.

Doh, Jonathan, Peter Rodriguez, Klaus Uhlenbruck, Jamie Collins and Lorraine Eden (2003). "Coping with corruption in foreign markets", *Academy of Management Executive*, 17(3), pp. 114-127.

Dunning, John and Alison McKaig-Berliner (2002). "The geographical sources of competitiveness: the professional business service industry", *Transnational Corporations*, 11(3), pp. 1-38.

Fankhauser, Sam and Lucia Lavric (2003). "The investment climate for climate investment: joint implementation in transition countries" (London: EBRD), mimeo.

Gilbert, Alyssa, Jan-Willem Bode and Dian Phylipsen (2004). *Analysis of the National Allocation Plans for the EU Emission Trading Scheme* (London: Ecofys UK).

Government of Brazil (2004). *Brasil's Initial National Communication to the United Nations Framework Convention on Climate Change* (Brasilia: Ministry of Science and Technology).

Government of China (2004). *The People's Republic of China Initial National Communication on Climate Change: Executive Summary*. Downloaded from the China Climate Change Info-Net at www.ccchina.gov.cn/english/source/da/da2004110901.pdf.

Government of India (2004). *India's Initial National Communication to the United Nations Framework Convention on Climate Change* (New Delhi: Ministry of Environment and Forests).

Hansen, Michael (2003). "Managing the environment across borders: a survey of environmental management in transnational corporations in Asia", *Transnational Corporations*, 12(1), pp. 27-52.

International Energy Agency (IEA) (2003). *World Energy Investment Outlook: 2003 Insights* (Paris: OECD/IEA).

International Emissions Trading Association (IETA) (2003). *Greenhouse Gas Market 2003: Emerging, but Fragmented* (Geneva: IETA).

Indian Planning Commission (2002). *Energy and the Environment, in the Government of India Planning Commission: Report of the Committee on India Vision 2020* (New Delhi: Planning Commission, Government of India). http://planningcommission.nic.in/reports/genrep/pl_vsn2020.pdf, last accessed on 12 January 2004.

Innovest (2001). *Uncovering Hidden Value Potential for Strategic Investors: The Automotive Industry* (New York: Innovest Strategic Value Investors).

Ito, Yoshiaki (2004). Personal communication, 30 April.

Jahn, Michael, Axel Michaelowa, Stefan Raubenheimer and Holger Liptow (2004). "Measuring the potential of unilateral CDM: a pilot study" (Hamburg: HWWA), mimeo.

Jiang, Xiaojuan (2001). "The new regional patterns of FDI inflow: policy orientation and the expected performance". Paper presented at the OECD-China Conference "Foreign Investment in China's Regional Development: Prospects and Policy Challenges", Xi'an, China, 11-12 October.

Jotzo, Frank, and Axel Michaelowa (2002). "Estimating the CDM market under the Marrakech Accords", *Climate Policy*, 2, pp. 179-196.

Komai, Toru (2004). Personal communication, 30 April.

Kumar, Nagesh (1996). "Foreign direct investments and technology transfers in development: a perspective on recent literature" (Maastricht: United Nations University), Institute for New Technologies Discussion Paper 9606, mimeo.

Lecocq, Frank (2004). *State and Trends of the Carbon Market 2004* (Washington, DC: PCF*plus* Research).

Lecocq, Frank and Karan Capoor (2003): *State and Trends of the Carbon Market 2003* (Washington, DC: PCF*plus* Research).

Li, Shaomin (2004). "Poor governance does not repel investors", *Foreign Direct Investment,* February/March. (www.fdimagazine.com/news/fullstory.php/aid/585/Poor_governance_does_not_repel_investors.html).

Lopes, Ignez Vidigal (2002). "Clean development mechanism (CDM): orientation guide" (Rio de Janeiro: Fundação Getulio Vargas), mimeo.

Michaelowa, Axel, Asuka Jusen, Karsten Krause, Bernhard Grimm and Tobias Koch (2003). "CDM projects in China's energy supply and demand sectors: opportunities and barriers", in Paul Harris, ed., *Global Warming and East Asia* (London: Routledge), pp. 109-132.

Miguez, José Domingos Gonzalez (2004). Personal communication, 8 November.

Morera, Liana, Olga Cabeza and Thomas Black-Arbeláez (2004). "The state of development of national (CDM) offices in Central and South America", in *Greenhouse Gas Emissions Trading and Project-based Mechanisms* (Paris: OECD), pp 31-51.

Natsource (2003): "Governments as participants in international markets for greenhouse gas commodities". Study prepared for IEA/IETA/EPRI/IDDRI, mimeo.

Organisation for Economic Co-operation and Development (OECD) (2003). "Conclusions and proposals for action". Paper presented at the International Conference on Trade and Investment: Maximising the Benefits of Globalisation for Africa (www.investrade-inafrica.org/EN/conclusion.htm).

_____ (2002). "Foreign direct investment for development: maximising benefits, minimising costs", in *OECD Policy Brief* (Paris: OECD).

_____(2001). *Environmental Priorities for China's Sustainable Development* (Paris: OECD).

Point Carbon (2004). "CDM host country rating update: China moves up, Mexico down", *Point Carbon news.*

Saggi, Kamal (2000) "*Trade, foreign direct investment and international technology transfer: a survey*" (Washington DC, The World Bank), mimeo.

Saner, Raymond, Serio Jáuregui and Lichia Yiu (2001). *Climate Change and Environmental Negotiations: Global and Local Dynamics. Reflections from Bolivia* (La Paz: Los Amigos del Libro).

Springer, Urs (2003). "The market for tradable GHG permits under the Kyoto Protocol: a survey of model studies", *Energy Economics,* 25, pp. 527-551.

Springer, Urs and Matthew Varilek (2004). "Estimating the price of tradable permits for greenhouse gas emissions in 2008–12", *Energy Policy,* 32, pp. 611–621.

United Nations Conference on Trade and Development (UNCTAD) (2004). *World Investment Report 2004: The Shift Towards Services,* (Geneva: United Nations).

_____(UNCTAD) (2003a). *World Investment Report 2003. FDI Policies for Development: National and International Perspectives* (Geneva: United Nations).

_____(UNCTAD) (2003b). *FDI in Brief: Brasil.* UNCTAD (r0.unctad.org/en/subsites/dite/fdistats_files/pdfs/wid_ib_ br_en.pdf).

_____(UNCTAD) (1998). *World Investment Report 1998: Trends and Determinants* (Geneva: United Nations).

United Nations Industrial Development Organization (UNIDO) (2003). *CDM Investor Guide Brazil* (Vienna: UNIDO).

World Business Council for Sustainable Development (WBCSD) (2004). *Engaging the Private Sector in the Clean Development Mechanism* (Geneva: WBCSD).

Woicke, Peter (2004). "Global goals. foreign direct investment", *Foreign Direct Investment,* January 2004 (www.fdimagazine.com/news/fullstory.php/aid/500/Global_goals.html).

World Bank, forthcoming. *National Strategy Study for India* (Washington, D.C.: World Bank).

_____ (2004). *Clean Development Mechanism in China: Taking a Proactive and Sustainable Approach*, 2nd Edition (Washington, DC: The World Bank).

The impact of China's FDI surge on FDI in South-East Asia: panel data analysis for 1986-2001

Yuping Zhou and Sanjaya Lall[*]

China's surge in foreign direct investment inflows is raising concerns that it is taking such investment away from other South-East Asian economies. This article assesses whether this is the case, using fixed-effects estimation to test for the relationships between FDI in South-East Asian economies within a simple model of location determinants of foreign direct investment, assuming the supply of FDI to be elastic. The results suggest that China raised rather than diverted such investment into neighbouring economies during 1986-2001; the results obtain whether inflows are lagged or not. This may be because countries do not compete for foreign direct investment in market and resource-seeking activities; the only competitive segment is likely to be export-processing – here China may be complementing other countries in electronics, where they are being integrated into a regional production network. There may be FDI substitution in other export-oriented industries, but the effect is not large enough to influence the results. However, the data do not allow different types of FDI to be tested separately, and this conclusion remains speculative.

Key Words: FDI, China, South-East Asia

[*] Yuping Zhou is an associate professor of economics at the Wuhan University of Technology in China; at the time of preparing this article, she was visiting research fellow at University of Oxford. Sanjaya Lall is Professor of Development Economics at the University of Oxford. We are grateful to John Weiss, research director of the Asian Development Bank Institute, for discussions and to three anonymous referees of this journal for valuable comments. We also thank Erol Taymaz, Pippa Biggs, Anna Lukyanova and Fuqiang He for advice on statistical methods. We alone are responsible for the contents of this article. Contact: sanjaya.lall@economics.oxford.ac.uk.

1. Introduction

In 2002, China surpassed the United States as a foreign direct investment (FDI) destination for the first time and, with an inflow of $53 billion, became the largest recipient of FDI in the world. In 1990, the other countries of South-East Asia[1] attracted four times as much FDI as China; today the opposite is true (figure 1). China's FDI surge is raising concerns among its regional neighbours,[2] most of which depend heavily on transnational corporations (TNCs) to drive their industrial, services and export growth. Since the signs are that China will continue to attract large FDI inflows, most neighbours fear that their inflows are under threat of substitution by China;[3] the threat is very similar to the one in manufactured exports, on which similar concerns have been raised.[4]

Figure 1. FDI inflows to South-East Asia and China, 1990 and 2002
(Billion dollars)

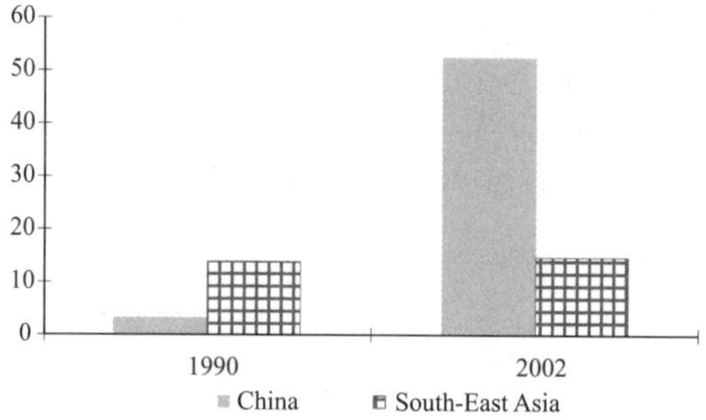

Source: UNCTAD, 2003.

[1] South-East Asia is taken here to include Indonesia, the Republic of Korea, Malaysia, Philippines, Singapore, Taiwan Province of China and Thailand. The FDI data are taken from different editions of UNCTAD's *World Investment Report*.

[2] The neighbours are described collectively as "South-East Asia" and include all developing and newly industrializing economies in East and South-East Asia. However, the statistical analysis in this article is confined to the major FDI recipients, described below.

[3] Chantasasawat *et al.* (2003) cite several comments by political leaders and analysts in South-East Asia on the threat to FDI inflows posed by China.

[4] On the Chinese threat to East Asian manufactured exports, see Lall and Albaladejo (2004).

While fears of a Chinese "threat" to FDI inflows are understandable, it is not clear that they are justified. The supply of FDI to the region is not strictly limited. Whether or not countries compete for FDI depends on the nature of the investment: a large portion of FDI flows into activities that do not actually compete with each other. There may still be FDI substitution by China, but it should be considered in an analytical framework that takes the other determinants of FDI location into account.

The article analyzes econometrically the relationship between FDI in China and other major recipients in the region. Section 2 describes China's FDI performance; section 3 discusses what "FDI competition" means; section 4 presents the statistical methodology; section 5 gives the results; and section 6 concludes.

2. Background

FDI inflows to China in 2002 were 28 times higher than in 1986, and its share of global FDI inflows increased from 1.4% to 8.1% over this period. China's large and fast growing market, cheap and productive labour, large pool of technical skills, growing export competitiveness and accession to WTO all increased TNC interest in locating operations there. In addition, China greatly liberalized its FDI regime over time, opening up various activities to foreign ownership; with greater liberalization of FDI in services following WTO accession, opportunities for foreign investors are likely to grow significantly.

Figure 2 shows the value of annual FDI inflows, and illustrates a clear break after 1991. FDI jumped by 244 % in 1992 as compared to 1991, and grew rapidly until 1997, when the financial crisis in the region slowed inflows (largely as a "contagion effect" from its neighbours, since China, with a tightly controlled capital account, did not itself fall into crisis). Inflows revived in 2000, and have since resumed their growth.

Figure 2. FDI inflows to China, 1986-2002
(Billion dollars)

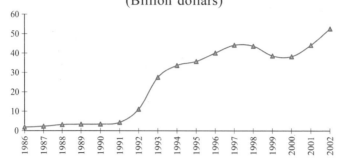

Source: UNCTAD, 2003.

Figure 3 shows FDI inflows into China as compared to South-East Asia,[5] and figure 4 the share of South-East Asian countries in global FDI inflows over 1986-2002. Both figures illustrate why China's neighbours feel threatened, particularly after 1992: while China's global FDI share rose steadily, that of most regional neighbours declined after 1991.

Figure 3. FDI flows to South-East Asia, 1992, 2002
(Billion dollars)

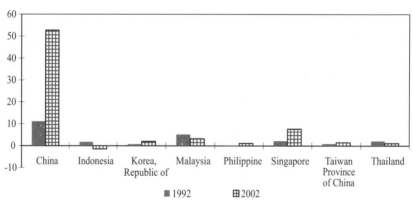

Source: UNCTAD, 2003.

---

[5] In 2002, FDI in China was 49.3 times larger than that in Thailand, 47.4 times larger than that in the Philippines, 26.7 times larger than that in the Republic of Korea, 16.5 times larger than that in Malaysia and 6.9 times larger than that in Singapore.

Figure 4. Share of South-East Asian countries in global inward FDI flows, 1986, 1992, 2002
(Per cent)

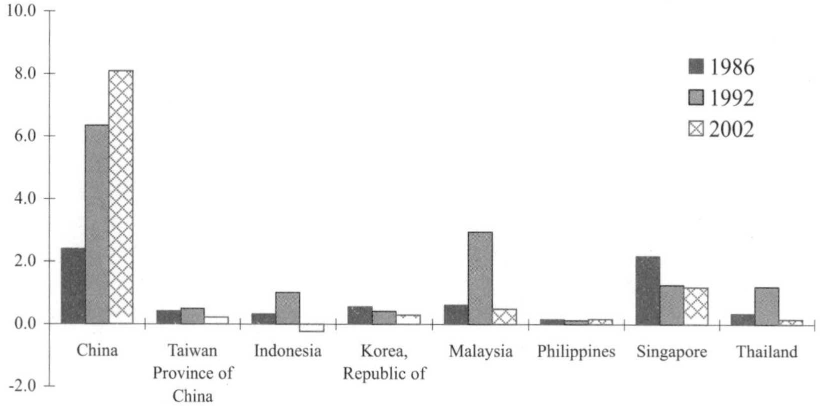

Source: UNCTAD, 2003.

We do not include Hong Kong, China in these figures or in the statistical analysis. This is for two reasons: first, a large part of FDI in Hong Kong, China is destined for China, and it is difficult to separate the two. Second, part of FDI from Hong Kong, China to China actually comes from the latter ("round-tripping" by mainland enterprises to evade taxes and other restrictions[6]). Both factors make the Hong Kong, China data volatile and unreliable.

While the absolute value of FDI inflows into China is impressive, it is much less so in per capita terms. The per capita FDI inflow to China in 2002 was lower than in Singapore (which is exceptionally high in the region), Malaysia, Taiwan Province

---

[6] Capital is moved out of China by a variety of mechanisms including transfer pricing, the establishment of holding companies in Hong Kong, China and tax havens by enterprises in China, and informal payment flows and cash outflows between the mainland and Hong Kong, China. Statistics show that tax haven economies were both one of the largest recipients and sources of FDI related to Hong Kong, China during 1998-2000. Perhaps much as 40 % of total FDI inflows to Hong Kong, China in 1998 was "Hong Kong-tax haven routing". It is now interwoven with the "mainland-Hong Kong round-tripping" (UNCTAD, 2001).

of China and the Republic of Korea (figure 5). However, China had surpassed Thailand, the Philippines and Indonesia, all of which were suffering the after-effects of the financial crisis. The relatively low value of China's per capita FDI may reinforce fears of a threat in that it still has some way to go before it reaches "normal" levels.

Figure 5. Per capita FDI flows to South-East Asia, 1986-2002

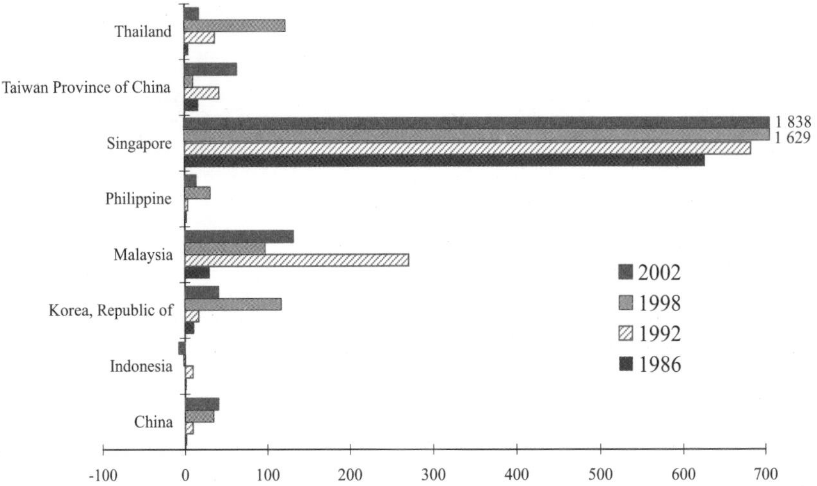

Sources: UNCTAD, 2003 and World Bank, World Development Indicators, 2003.

FDI in China is concentrated in manufacturing, which accounted for nearly 70% of total inflows by 2002 (table 1). The primary sector (agriculture and mining) accounted for only 3% in that year, with services, including R&D, accounting for the remainder.

The sectoral pattern of FDI in China has changed over the past 20 years, shifting from labour-intensive activities in the 1980s to capital and technology-intensive ones in the 1990s (Lemoine and Unal-Kesenci, 2002). One aspect of importance is the growing focus of FDI on high technology products, particularly (but not only) for export. TNCs' electronics exports (the main products in the hi-technology category) from China increased from $4.5 billion in 1996 to $29.8 billion in 2000 (*ibid.*), and accounted in the latter year for one-fourth of exports by foreign affiliates and 81% of China's exports of high-technology products (UNCTAD, 2002).

Table 1. Shares of utilized FDI, by sector and industry, 2000-2002
(Per cent)

Sector	2000	2001	2002
Farming, forestry, animal husbandry and fisheries	1.66	1.92	1.95
Mining and quarrying	1.43	1.73	1.10
Manufacturing	63.48	65.93	69.77
Electricity, gas and water	5.51	4.85	2.61
Construction	2.22	1.72	1.34
Geological prospecting	0.01	0.02	0.01
Transport, storage, post and telecommunication services	2.49	1.94	1.73
Wholesale and retail trade and catering	2.11	2.49	1.77
Banking and insurance	0.19	0.08	0.20
Real estate management	11.44	10.96	10.74
Social services	5.37	5.54	5.58
Health care, sports and social welfare	0.26	0.25	0.24
Education, culture and arts, radio, film and television	0.13	0.08	0.07
Research and development services	0.14	0.26	0.37
Other	3.57	2.24	2.50

Source: National Bureau of Statistics of China, *China Statistical Yearbook* (2003).

The significance of electronics exports for this article is that TNCs are integrating China into a close-knit production and export network spanning much of East Asia (Lall, Albaladejo and Zhang, 2004),[7] making the region the world's leading base

---

[7] See UNCTAD, 2002; Ernst and Kim, 2002; Hobday, 2001; Lall, Albaladejo and Zhang, 2004. However, two leading East Asian exporters, the Republic of Korea and Taiwan Province of China, are integrated into global production systems in a different way from the other countries, relying more on arm's length subcontracting relations with developed country TNCs. However, their national firms are major TNCs in their own right and are building global production networks that encompass China and other South-East Asian countries.

for assembly, testing, integrated production and, increasingly, research and development (R&D). While TNCs also dominate some other export activities in the region, they have not developed similar integrated systems. The reason lies in the ease of transportability and high value of electronic products, along with their need for labour-intensive assembly and testing, which make them eminently suitable for segmentation of functions and processes across countries (*ibid.*). This raises the possibility that FDI in electronics is complementary across countries in the production network, with growing capacities in one country stimulating similar capacities in others.

Studies are starting to appear on FDI "diversion" by China. The two known to the present authors conclude that China does not pose a competitive threat to the region. F. Wu and P. K. Keong (2002), in a qualitative analysis of FDI flows to East Asia, conclude that much of the growth in FDI in China was due to increased FDI from Hong Kong, China and did not detract FDI from ASEAN. However, this analysis is fairly impressionistic and lacks a proper analytical framework to analyse FDI substitution.

C. Busakorn *et al.* (2003) use econometric analysis to test whether China diverts FDI from eight South-East Asian economy.[8] They regress annual FDI inflows in the eight countries on a set of location determinants of FDI, using FDI to China as an independent variable. They find that FDI in China is positively related to *levels* of FDI in these other economies but negatively to their *shares* in total FDI in Asia and total FDI in developing countries. This article is the closest to our analysis and reaches similar conclusions; however, there are some problems with the methodology used, to which we turn later.

---

[8] The eight economies are Hong Kong, China, Taiwan Province of China, the Republic of Korea, Singapore, Malaysia, the Philippines, Indonesia and Thailand. Our analysis also uses these economies with the exception of Hong Kong, China.

3. Defining "FDI competition"

When do countries "compete" for FDI? The most obvious case for any resource flow is when the available amount of the resource in question is limited; in the extreme case, greater flows to one country reduces flows to others by the same amount. This "zero-sum" definition is difficult to justify for FDI: the amount of FDI available is not fixed. At the global level, FDI forms only 12 % of global gross domestic capital formation (UNCTAD, 2003), and additional resources can easily be added should investment opportunities arise, from domestic resources or other international capital flows (e.g. portfolio investment). While annual FDI flows fluctuate widely in response to changes in the investment climate and stock market performance, business cycles, non-economic events (wars and the like) and shifts in investment opportunities, the *supply of investible funds* does not normally appear as a major determinant of FDI. [9]

At a regional level, in East Asia there is even less reason to expect investible resources to be limited. This region accounted for only 16% of global inward FDI flows over 1986-2002 (14% in 2002). In any case, TNCs do not allocate investment on a regional basis – say, allow only a given sum for East Asia – and so forego profitable opportunities in one country there because they have already invested in its neighbour (i.e. used up their regional quota). Even if one TNC were unable to undertake an investment at a given time because of resource constraints, in most industries there would be several others that would seize a promising opportunity within a short period. Over the medium term, therefore, there is little reason to expect FDI in the region to be supply-constrained. [10]

---

[9] Zhan (2002) has a good analysis of the different implications of competition for FDI, focusing on policy measures used to attract FDI. Chantasasawat *et al.* (2003) do not discuss the concept of "FDI competition", simply using FDI in China as an independent variable in a model of FDI location.

[10] This assumes that the investment climate in all the countries is equally attractive, in terms of political and economic stability, FDI regulations, legal systems and so on. While these do differ within South-East Asia – Indonesia, in particular, has suffered from a deteriorating climate since the financial crisis of 1997 – in general this is not a major factor differentiating East Asian countries and we abstract from it here.

However, there may be "FDI competition" even with an elastic supply of investible resources. Its nature and incidence will depend on whether FDI in one country pre-empts that in another due to market rather than resource constraints. Consider this for the four main types of FDI (following the classification developed by Dunning, 1993):

- *Market-seeking FDI*, determined by the size, growth and attractiveness of the domestic market in a host country and its investment climate, does not incur competition across countries. While China offers attractive investment opportunities, this does not *per se* "threaten" its neighbours if their markets are also attractive. One of the main areas of FDI activity in this category is services, and there is no indication that there is substitution in investment between countries here.

- *Resource-seeking FDI* is similar to market-seeking FDI, and does not induce substitution between countries. In any case, China is not a resource-rich country by normal standards and, as table 1 shows, does not receive much FDI in resource-based activities. It is therefore unlikely to threaten resource-seeking investments in neighbours like Indonesia.

- *Asset-seeking FDI*, searching for resources that can add to TNCs' advantages (e.g. new technology or skills) is not relevant to most of the East Asian region (though the Republic of Korea and Taiwan Province of China are emerging as innovators) and has not been an important determinant of FDI there. In any case, asset-seeking FDI also does not result in country-specific competition.

- *Efficiency-seeking FDI*, where TNCs invest to serve external markets, is where direct competition is most likely. Since the number of export-oriented facilities worldwide in any industry is given by the size of the market, one country can potentially pre-empt another by attracting TNC facilities. However, a vital caveat is that, in integrated production networks, FDI in one country may lead to greater FDI in another.[11] Countries in South-East Asia offer different operating environments for efficiency-seeking FDI: apart from different wage levels, they have different levels of skills, technology, supplier development, infrastructure, logistical facilities and support institutions.[12] Thus, TNCs spread their production networks over countries in response to differences in such factors, fitting them into a complex production hierarchy to optimise overall efficiency.[13] The electronics industry is particularly prone to FDI complementarity in this region.

[11] FDI complementarity may also arise in other circumstances. For instance, it may lead to higher demand for imported raw materials and so lead to greater FDI in primary producers (Latin America may benefit from growth in China in this way, and some of the FDI will come from China itself). Or FDI may lead, via higher incomes in China, to greater demand for various new exports by other countries and so to FDI in relevant industries.

[12] Incentives may also make a difference, at least in the short term, but as they are unlikely to matter significantly over the long term, we ignore them here.

[13] Industries differ in the extent to which they can be integrated into production networks (and so be complementary), depending on technological characteristics. Some industries have highly fragmentable processes (Arndt and Kierzkowski, 2000; Lall, Albaladejo and Zhang, 2004): production can be separated into discrete stages, with different processes placed in different countries. The most fragmentable activities are engineering-based, like machinery, automobiles and electronics. The least fragmentable are activities with continuous processes like chemicals, paper or food processing; here it is not possible to break production up and locate segments in different countries to take advantage of fine cost differences, though some functions like R&D, back-office services and logistics can be relocated (see UNCTAD, 2004). Even engineering industries differ in the extent to which they can be fragmented. The degree of fragmentation depends on the value-to-weight ratio of the product (light, high value products can be transported long distances to take advantage of small differences in production costs, while heavy, low value ones cannot) and the skill needs of processes (only those with relatively simple processes can relocate to low wage, low skill countries). The industry most prone to fragmentation is electronics: it has light, high-value products and simple final assembly processes. Heavy machinery and automobiles fragment to a lesser extent because products are heavier and skill needs more demanding (Lall, Albaladejo and Zhang, 2004).

A significant part of FDI in the region, depending on the country, is market seeking (reinforced by the recent growth of FDI in services), and in countries like Indonesia a large part is also resource-seeking; both sets are likely to be non-competing. In efficiency-seeking activities, significant for many countries in the region, there is more possibility of substitution, with the major exception being FDI in integrated systems, led by electronics. There is also cross-country specialization within other FDI-dependent export industries in the region, but there is less intense integration. Low-technology industries like textiles and apparel, footwear and toys *are* linked across countries, but the subdivision of activity is not as fine or as advanced as in electronics. The automotive industry, the other complex industry with integrated production systems, has not established a regional production system in East Asia in the way that it has in parts of Latin America (Lall, Albaladejo and Zhang, 2004). It is likely, therefore, that there is more direct competition for FDI in other export-oriented activities than in electronics.

Ideally, our analysis should have tested for the impact of Chinese FDI for each major category of FDI (and for each major export-oriented activity) separately. However, data are only available for total FDI for most countries (though some, like Malaysia, also give industrial breakdown for FDI approvals, though not for projects actually realized). Without comparable FDI data for all countries for each year by industry, however, we must confine the analysis to total FDI inflows. The exercise thus covers the whole range of competitive, non-competitive and complementary trends in different types of FDI, and the result is the net outcome of their interactions.

4. Methodology

We analyze the impact of FDI inflows to China on FDI in the following South-East Asian economies: Indonesia, Malaysia, Philippines, Republic of Korea, Singapore, Taiwan Province of China and Thailand. As control variables, we include major locational factors affecting FDI and a dummy variable for the impact of the 1997 financial crisis. We employ a panel data analysis to estimate the impact of these variables, using data for the 16 years from 1986 to 2001. This provides 99 observations in total, along with sub-period data with 42 observations for 1986-1991 and 66 for 1992-2001. The panel data analysis allows us to control for country-specific effects in estimating how FDI flows are determined. Fixed-effects estimation enables us to analyse the relationship among different economies over time (Kevin, 2001). We use the following specification:

$$\text{lnper capita FDI}_{it} = \beta_i + \ddot{a}\ln X_{it} + \mathring{a}_{it} D_{it} + u_{it}, \quad (1)$$

where the subscripts "i" and "t" stand for country I and period t; X_{it} is a set of FDI determinants for inward FDI of country i at time t; per capita FDI_{it}, total FDI divided by population, indicates FDI flows into the ith economy in year t, and X_{it} denotes the independent variables which vary across economies and over time. X_i represents per capita FDI in China, GDP, per capita GDP, per capita stock of FDI and economy-specific effects are captured by β_i. D_{it} indicates that dummy variables are employed to estimate how the Asian financial crisis influenced FDI flows. u_{it} is a random disturbance. Data on FDI, population and GDP are taken from UNCTAD's *World Investment Report 2003*. All variables are converted to logs.

a. Variables

Dependent variable. To test for the impact of China's FDI inflows, we measure FDI in per capita rather than absolute terms. Absolute FDI would give a distorted picture as it would be dominated by the size of the economy, a particular problem when comparing relatively small countries with a giant like China. As noted, we cannot predict whether FDI flows are competitive, non-competitive or complementary.

Independent variables.

FDI in China, measured in per capita terms, is the main variable of interest here. However, to capture its true impact we use a number of variables to capture the other main determinants of inward FDI.

Market size, measured by total GDP, is widely considered a key factor in attracting FDI (Globerman and Shapiro, 2002; Dunning, 1993; Chandprapalert, 2000). The theoretical link between the size of GDP and FDI inflows is clear: a larger market lowers distribution and information costs when production and distribution facilities are established in a market, and a clustering of other producers and suppliers in a large market creates or accentuates agglomeration economies. However, most models of FDI location test for the effect of market size on the absolute value of FDI inflows; as we use per capita FDI as the dependent variable, our results may not be comparable to those of others. Market size may affect the level of per capita FDI but not its change from year to year.

Per capita GDP is used as an indicator of the sophistication and differentiation of a market – and so for demand for the advanced and differentiated products in which TNCs often have advantages – as well as of some other factors that affect FDI flows, e.g. the level of skills, infrastructure, institutions, legal systems and so on. Several empirical studies have found, as expected, a significant and positive relationship between per capita GDP and FDI.[14] For instance, V.N. Bandera and J.T. White (1968), using pooled data on United States manufacturing FDI in seven European economies over the period 1958-1962, strongly support the hypothesized dependency of the level of FDI (but not the first order change in FDI) on the level of national income in a host country. P. Tsai (1994), in an econometric analysis of a non-linear simultaneous equations model using pooled aggregate data for 62 countries over the period 1975-1978 and for 51 countries over the period 1983-1986, finds that higher per capita GDP is associated with a higher level of inward FDI.

The per capita stock of FDI is used to capture the general investment climate for FDI. A large existing stock of FDI is taken as evidence that a country has a good regime for foreign investors (i.e. stability, low regulations, appropriate taxes, other

---

[14] See, for instance, Bandera and White, 1968; Lunn, 1980; Pain, 1993; Lucas, 1993 and Tsai, 1994.

economic factors affecting operations). While something of a "catch all" variable, it is appropriate for our purposes since our objective is not to comprehensively explain the location of FDI but to test for the impact of FDI in China. Since the investment climate for FDI has been relatively stable in the region, it meets our needs for a control variable rather well.

We include a dummy variable for the Asian financial crisis. In the second half of 1997, turmoil erupted in some South-East Asian economies. Large amounts of short-term capital left the most affected ones: Indonesia, the Republic of Korea, Malaysia, the Philippines and Thailand. However, FDI inflows remained positive; indeed, inflows in 1997 to these five countries together were similar to those of 1996. In 1998, however, they fell by 13.2 % (UNCTAD, 1998) and started to recover a year so later; however, Indonesia remained an outlier because of political instability and economic adjustment problems, and continued to suffer from low or negative inflows. Over the period as a whole, therefore, we do not expect a strong effect for this variable: we define D_{it} to equal one for 1997 and 1998, the years when the financial crisis was at its peak, and zero otherwise.

Let us conclude this section with a comparison of our model with that of A. Chantasasawat et al. (2003). The latter use the total value of FDI inflows as their dependent variable, while we use FDI per capita to control for the large size differences between China and its neighbours. They also use FDI shares in Asia and the developing world, but we do not as this is equivalent to assuming that FDI is a "zero sum game" – the rise in the share of China in Asia must be accompanied by a fall in that of other countries. It is not surprising, therefore, that Chantasasawat et al. (2003) find a negative impact of FDI in China for this dependent variable: this simply follows from the fact that FDI in China has grown faster than in its neighbours.

Chantasasawat et al. (2003) use many more explanatory variables than we do. They use GDP growth, import duties, trade openness, the illiteracy rate, the corporate tax rate, government stability, corruption, the average manufacturing wage, the number of telephone lines per 1,000 people and per capita GDP.

The rationale for some of these variables, and sometimes their measurement, are not convincing. The "openness" variable (exports plus imports/GDP) is dubious, for instance: many analysts distrust this measure because it captures country size, primary resources and a number of other factors apart from trade policy that affect it. The illiteracy rate is a weak indicator of the kind of human capital that is relevant to FDI. Corporate taxes are not sufficiently variable in the region to matter for long-term investments. Government stability and corruption are based on very subjective measures. There is little theoretical rationale for using the level of wages as a determinant of FDI: market and resource seeking FDI are not affected by this and export-oriented FDI is affected by overall efficiency rather than wages *per se*. The proxy for physical infrastructure is of dubious value.

We tried a few similar variables in early analysis but decided to drop them for lack of hard data or because of a weak theoretical rationale for the measure. We dropped GDP growth for a lack of significance. We did not use a trade regime variable since such regimes did not vary across the seven countries in the 1990s sufficiently to matter to foreign investors. We did use dummy variables to capture the impact of the financial crisis, while Chantasasawat *et al.* (2003) ignore this factor.

Finally, Chantasasawat *et al.* (2003) run their analysis for the whole period 1985-2001, but do not differentiate between periods before and after 1991, when there was a structural shift in FDI into China. We differentiate between 1986-1991 and 1992-2001 to capture this structural break.

b. Specifying the model

All variables are measured in logarithms to adjust for heteroskedasticity; thus, their coefficient measures the elasticity of FDI flows. To bring out possible structural variations over the period, separate estimations of the model are conducted for three periods: 1986-2001 as a whole, and 1986-1991 and 1992-2001 separately. The division into two sub-periods is undertaken to account for the possibility that foreign investors responded to changes in China's investment and trade environment.[15] In addition, we test each independent variable in current values as well as with a one-year lag to capture possible lags.

5. Estimation results

Both dependent and independent variables are computed by taking mean values of the variables over the relevant periods for each sub-period. The estimates of panel data for the full sample are conducted by the fixed effects approach. Tables 2 and 3 present parameter estimates from the panel estimates for the two sub-periods (1986-1991, 1992-2001) and from the panel data for the entire sample (1986-2001), using both current values (table 2) and with a one-year lag (table 3).

The overall performance of panel estimates in both models is satisfactory. The R^2 for all the estimates are fairly high, particularly for the panel estimates for the sub-periods 1986-1991 and 1992-2001. The relationships between the dependent variables and the independent variables in both formulations are strong, with the F-statistics significant at a 1% level in each model. On the whole, the lagged model works better than the current-value model.

Both the estimates for the whole period and for the sub-period 1986-1991 suggest that FDI inflows are *not* significantly related to FDI in China. The estimates for the sub-period 1992-2001, in both current and lagged terms, show a significant impact of Chinese FDI – with a *positive* sign (the estimates based on current values show higher complementarity that those based on lagged values). Thus, no estimate suggests that China is diverting FDI from the rest of the region; on the contrary, there

---

[15] The government of China launched an economic adjustment programme in the late 1988 to reduce rapidly rising inflation, leading to a halt in all new FDI projects. The crackdown on the student demonstration at the Tiananmen Square in 1989 affected FDI because foreign investors began to question Chinese political stability (Kevin, 2001). The milestone year in terms of Chinese FDI policies was 1991, when Deng Xiaoping opened up the economy significantly.

---

appears to be growing complementarity between China and its major neighbours after 1992 and no significant effect before this.

Table 2. Panel estimates of determinants of FDI inflows to South-East Asia (dependent variable: per capita FDI (current value))

Independent variables	1986-2001	1986-1991	1992-2001
ln per capita FDI in China (current $)	-0.5039 (0.109)	-1.3578 (0.529)	12.3868* (0.070)
ln GDP (current $)	-0.2846 (0.824)	5.1141 (0.167)	-3.9357 (0.116)
ln per capita GDP (current $ per capita)	0.2366 (0.852)	-5.0894 (0.166)	3.2339 (0.184)
ln per capita FDI inward stock (current $ per capita)	1.7849*** (0.003)	-1.3578 (0.172)	-31.6091* (0.092)
dum97	0.2673 (0.68)	-	-0.2843 (-0.80)
dum98	-0.1176 (-0.72)	-	-0.6172 (-1.61)
R^2 (overall)	0.4670	0.8200	0.7773
F-statistics	5.53	5.06	4.10

Source: the authors.
Notes: The number of observations for panel estimates is 108, and for panel estimates 1986-91, 1992-96 and 1997-2001 are 42 and 66, respectively. The data in parentheses show significance probabilities. The estimating results for constant terms are omitted to save space. The asterisks ***, **, and * indicate the levels of significance at the 1%, 5%, and 10% levels, respectively.

How can we explain this apparent complementarity?

• The complementarity may partly be only apparent rather than real: a large (possibly dominant) part of inward FDI in the region may be non-competing (market- and resource-seeking). Such FDI is rising in most countries in response to fast growth and ongoing liberalization, and is not causally related across countries, except indirectly in the sense that the region shares in dynamic spillover benefits and a better investment image.

• Different countries in South-East Asia are at different levels of development and offer different advantages to foreign investors. In fragmented industries, as noted, countries attract different processes and functions within similar industries, and so genuinely complement each other.

Table 3. Panel estimates of determinants of FDI inflows to South-East Asia (dependent variable: per capita FDI (one year lag))

Independent variables	1986-2001	1986-1991	1992-2001
ln per capita FDI in China-1	-0.1216	-6.1370	2.0726*
(current $)	(0.694)	(0.134)	(0.095)
ln GDP-1	-1.8931	8.2048*	-3.9264*
(current $)	(0.173)	(0.067)	(0.085)
ln per capita GDP-1	1.7541	-8.1935*	4.0176
(current $ per capita)	(0.202)	(0.066)	(0.107)
ln per capita FDI inward stock-1	1.1915**	5.5626*	-3.3692
(current $ per capita)	(0.046)	(0.085)	(0.210)
dum97	0.1692	-	-0.0433
	(0.2673)	-	(-0.6811)
dum98	-0.1947	-	-0.3903
	(-0.1176)	-	(-1.0293)
R^2 (overall)	0.8549	0.8890	0.7737
F-statistics	5.61	4.32	4.39

Source: the authors.
Notes: The number of observations for panel estimates is 101, and for panel estimate 1986-91 and 1992-2001 is 35 and 66 respectively. The data in parentheses refer to significance probabilities. The estimating results for constant terms are omitted to save space. The asterisks ***, **, and * indicate the levels of significance at the 1%, 5%, and 10% levels, respectively.

- The "flying geese pattern", a popular characterization of the pattern of intra-Asian FDI, explains part of the investment complementarity. As countries move up the development and industrialization ladder, they shift less advanced facilities to lower wage economies in the region. With Japan at the top, followed by the mature Asian Tigers (Singapore, Hong Kong, China, the Republic of Korea and Taiwan Province of China), ASEAN, China and finally other emerging economies, FDI is therefore flowing across the region in response to evolving comparative advantages (Sikorski and Menkhoff, 2000).

- A significant part of FDI in China comes from Taiwan Province of China and Hong Kong, China (table 4). Most of this FDI is unlikely to deprive other economies, since it depends heavily on the investors' "Chinese connection" (linguistic, cultural and family) and may not have gone to other economies in any case.

- Risk-diversification strategies may lead TNCs to invest in different countries in the region, even if one in particular (China) were the most efficient producer for a given product or component. They would be reluctant to place all critical facilities in China: it would be too risky (Lall and Albaladejo, 2004).

- "Round-tripping" of FDI between Hong Kong, China and the mainland, which, as noted, may account for a significant part of FDI in China, does not divert FDI from other regions.

Coming now to the other independent variables, *market size* does not affect FDI in South-East Asia when current values are used. However, the lagged panel and panel data estimates for the two sub-periods suggest that market size has varying effects on FDI, positive in 1986-2001 and 1986-1991 negative in 1992-2001, both at the 10% confidence level. The unexpected result for the latter period may reflect either the possibility that market size does not affect per capita FDI or reflect the impact of the Asian financial crisis.

Table 4. Sources of FDI in China 1992-1998
(Million dollars, per cent)

Economy/region	1992-1998	
	Total inflows	Per cent
Asian developing economies	**173,090**	**74.00**
Hong Kong, China	124,300	53.57
Taiwan Province of China	19,458	8.32
Singapore	11,626	4.97
Korea, Republic of	8,005	3.42
Thailand	1,620	0.69
Others	7,081	3.03
Developed economies	**60,816**	**25.99**
Japan	18,890	8.08
United States	17,963	7.68
United Kingdom	5,830	2.49
Germany	3,332	1.42
France	2,046	0.87
Canada	1,876	0.80
Netherlands	1,535	0.66
Others	9,344	3.99
Total	**233,906**	**100.00**

Sources: Data for 1992-1997 are from International Trade (various issues) by MOFERT. Others are from *Almanac of China's Foreign Economic Relations and Trade* (various issues) by MOFERT and *China Statistical Yearbook* (various years). All data for FDI flows and stocks are realized investment in current values.

Per capita GDP at current values does not affect FDI flows in South-East Asia, while the lagged values show different effects according to the period. As with total GDP, the effect is positive for the period as a whole, but differs by sub-periods, being positive during 1986-2001 and 1992-2001 and negative during 1986-1991 (significant at the 10% confidence level).

Per capita inward FDI stock has a positive effect on FDI flows in Southeast Asia in both specifications, and is significant at a 1% confidence level. In both specifications, per capita lagged FDI stock is significant and positively related to FDI inflows during 1986-1991, but negatively related during 1992-2001. It is not clear why this variable shows a negative coefficient in the latter period, but it may be picking up the delayed effects of the financial crisis that the dummy variables miss out.

The *dummy variables for the financial crisis* in 1997 and 1998 do not have significant effects on FDI flows in either model. This surprising result may be due to the inadequacy of the dummy variable as a measure, or to the effect of other variables that pick up the effects of the crisis, or perhaps that the negative effect on FDI over the medium term was largely confined to one country (Indonesia).

Our final result is similar to that of Chantasasawat *et al.* (2003) in that they also find that China's FDI complements FDI in the other economies (the results hold when, as with our model, Hong Kong, China is excluded). However, they find complementarity for the entire period while we find evidence of this only in the later period, i.e. we find *growing complementarity* over time – presumably the result of intensification of production networks. They also find that openness is highly significant, but given the nature of the measure employed, this finding is hard to interpret (high FDI may well be associated with greater trade due to other factors rather than to falling trade barriers). They find corporate tax rates to be significant, but not measures of corruption or stability. In general, their results support our conclusions.

6. Conclusions

While China's FDI surge has raised concerns in the region, our analysis suggests that much of the concern is unfounded. China does not seem to have crowded out FDI inflows to other countries. On the contrary, China is either not competing with them for FDI or is actually stimulating complementary investments in them. It is difficult to separate out the two effects (non-competing investments and complementarity). This does not imply, however, that there is *no* competition between China and its neighbours for FDI in all activities or that complementarity will continue to grow.

There are likely to be export-oriented activities where FDI in China deprives neighbours of foreign-owned facilities, or where more rapid expansion in China means lower growth in a neighbour. This is likely to be true of most export activities not organised in integrated systems, such as textiles and clothing, footwear, or toys. The substitution effect may grow over time as Chinese industrial capabilities (skills, technology levels, supplier bases, infrastructure) improve and its large market size allows it to reap scale and scope economies out of reach of its neighbours. There may also be growing substitution within electronics production networks, if China's growing capabilities lead TNCs to locate more or higher quality facilities there. However, these conjectures must remain speculative in the absence of better industry-level evidence.

Even if its neighbours become less competitive than China in traded activities, this may not lead to falls in overall FDI levels. TNCs may well invest in China's neighbours in domestic-market-oriented activities like services: the net effect on FDI will depend on how large and dynamic these other activities are. The main policy concern should not be about FDI flows as much as about building the capabilities to maintain growth in activities that remain competitive in the face of the Chinese challenge. ∎

References

Arndt, S. W. and H. Kierzkowski, ed., (2001). *Fragmentation: New Production Patterns in the World Economy* (Oxford: Oxford University Press).

Bandera, V.N. and J.T. White (1968). "U.S. direct investments and domestic markets in Europe", *Economia Internazionale,* 21, pp. 117-133.

Busakorn C., K.C. Fung, I. Hitomi and S. Alan (2003). "International competition for foreign direct investment: the case of China", Santa Cruz: University of California, mimeo.

Chandprapalert, A (2000). "The determinants of U.S. direct investment in Thailand: a survey on managerial perspectives", *Multinational Business Review*, 8 (2), pp. 82-88.

Dunning, J. H. (1993). *Multinational Enterprises and the Global Economy* (New York: Addison-Wesley).

Ernst, D. and L. Kim (2002). "Global production networks, knowledge diffusion and local capability formation", *Research Policy*, 31, pp. 1417-1429.

Hobday, M. G. (2001). "The electronics industries of Pacific Asia: exploiting international production networks for economic development", *Asia Pacific Economic Literature*, 15(1), pp. 13-29.

Globerman, S and D. Shapiro (2002). "Global foreign direct investment flows: the role of governance infrastructure", *World Development*, 30(11), pp. 1899-1919.

Lall, S. and M. Albaladejo (2004). "China's competitive performance: a threat to East Asian manufactured exports? " *World Development*, 32(9), pp. 1441-1466.

_____ and J. Zhang (2004). "Mapping fragmentation: electronics and automobiles in East Asia and Latin America", *Oxford Development Studies*, 32 (3), pp. 407-432.

Lemoine, F. and D. Unal-Kesenci (2002). "China in the international segmentation of production processes" (Paris: *Centre d'Etude Prospectives et d'Informations Internationale*, CEPII Working Paper No. 2002-02), mimeo.

Lucas, R. E. B. (1993). "On the determinants of direct foreign investment: evidence from East and Southeast Asia", *World Development*, 21, pp. 391-406.

Lunn, J. (1980). "Determinants of US direct investment in the EEC", *European Economic Review*, 13, pp. 93-101.

Pain, N. (1993). "An econometric analysis of foreign direct investment in the United Kingdom", *Scottish Journal of Political Economy*, 40, pp. 1-23.

Sikorski, D. and T. Mennkhoff (2000). "Internationalization of Asian business", *Singapore Management Review*, 22, pp. 1-17.

Tsai, P. (1994). "Determinants of foreign direct investment and its impact on economic growth", *Journal of Economic Development*, 19, pp. 137-163.

United Nations Conference on Trade and Development (UNCTAD) (2004). *World Investment Report 2004: FDI in Services* (New York and Geneva: United Nations).

_____ (2003). *World Investment Report 2003: FDI Policies for Development: National and International Perspectives* (New York and Geneva: United Nations).

_____ (2002). *World Investment Report 2002: TNCs and Export Competitiveness* (New York and Geneva: United Nations).

_____ (2001). *World Investment Report 2001: Promoting Linkages* (New York and Geneva: United Nations).

_____ (1998). *World Investment Report 1998: Trends and Determinants* (New York and Geneva: United Nations).

Wu, F. and P. K. Keong (2002). "Foreign direct investment to China and Southeast Asia: has ASEAN been losing out?" *Journal of Asian Business*, 18 (3), pp. 45-59.

Zhan, J. (2002). "Policy competition for FDI: to what extent does it make sense?" (Geneva: UNCTAD), mimeo.

Zhang, K. H. (2001). "What attracts foreign multinational corporations to China?" *Contemporary Economic Policy*, 19, pp. 336-346.

The determinants of liberalization of FDI policy in developing countries: a cross-sectional analysis, 1992-2001

Stephen J. Kobrin*

The decade of the 1990s was characterized by widespread liberalization of laws and regulations affecting inflows of foreign direct investment in developing countries. Using a data base supplied by UNCTAD, this article employs a cross-sectional regression methodology to analyze the determinants of liberalization of foreign direct investment policies in 116 developing countries from 1992 to 2001. Ninety-five per cent of the changes in such policies over the decade (1,029 of 1,086) were liberalizing rather than restrictive. Two possible explanations of liberalization are suggested: policy makers' beliefs that attracting more foreign direct investment is in the best interests of their countries, and external pressure to adopt neoliberal economic policies either from the dominant power (the United States) or international organizations such as the World Bank or International Monetary Fund. Results provide strong support for the "rational" decision (or "opportunity costs of closure") argument and only limited support for the external pressure thesis. Country size, level of human resource capabilities and trade openness are found to be the primary determinants of the propensity to liberalize.

* William H. Wurster Professor of Multinational Management, Department of Management, The Wharton School, University of Pennsylvania. Todor Enev and Xun Wu provided research assistance. The Reginald Jones Center at the Wharton School supported this project. The data were provided generously by the Division of Investment, Technology, and Enterprise Development at UNCTAD. The author would like to thank three anonymous referees as well as Mauro Guillen, Edward Mansfield, Karl P. Sauvant and Vitold Henisz for comments on a previous draft. Contact: kobrins@wharton.upenn.edu.

Introduction

The 1991 *World Development Report* (World Bank, 1991, p. 31) concluded that a "sea change" had taken place in thinking about development: by the late 1980s, many developing countries had moved away from State directed, inwardly focused strategies towards an acceptance of both markets and integration into the world economy. While the motivations for this marked shift in policy are complex, the failure of import substitution, the success of the relatively open Asian economies, the collapse of socialism as an alternative, and the economic crises of the 1980s all played a role (Millner, 1999).

In 1990 John Williamson concluded that there was a "Washington Consensus" about the desirability of openness to the world economy, liberalization of domestic markets and macroeconomic stability (Gore, 2000; Williamson, 2000). In a retrospective article, he argues that "my version of the Washington Consensus can be seen as an attempt to summarize the policies that were widely viewed as supportive of development at the end of two decades when economists had become convinced that the key to rapid economic development lay not in a country's natural resources or even in its physical or human capital, but rather in the set of economic policies that it pursued" (Williamson 2000, p. 254).

Williamson believed that the process of intellectual convergence after the collapse of communism was reflected in ten economic rerforms: the seventh was liberalization of flows of foreign direct investment (FDI).[1] He wrote at the start of a period characterized by the widespread liberalization of laws and regulations affecting flows of both portfolio capital and FDI (Brune *et al.*, 2001).[2] While developing countries began to

---

[1] Williamson *did not* call for full capital account liberalization.

[2] Brune *et al.* found that there were no aggregate increases in capital account openness in low and middle income countries until 1991. After that point there was a period of rapid and dramatic liberalization (Brune et al., 2001). Also see Barry Eichengreen (2001) and International Monetary Fund (2001), especially chapter 4, "International financial integration and developing countries".

reduce or remove restrictions on FDI during the 1980s, the trend became pronounced and widespread during the early 1990s as increasing numbers of policy makers came to believe that integration into the world economy was a prerequisite to growth and development and that FDI from transnational corporations (TNCs) was the vehicle to accomplish that end.[3]

A number of factors led to increased efforts by developing countries to attract flows of FDI. First, there was increased recognition by policy makers that the bundle of assets and capabilities encompassed in FDI could contribute directly to growth and development of the national economy. Second, declining levels of other forms of assistance increased reliance on FDI, and various financial crises may have led to a preference for longer term, relatively stable and often tangible flows of direct investment. Last, developing country governments have gained confidence in their ability to maximize the benefits and minimize the liabilities of investment by TNCs (UNCTAD, 1994, p. 85). As a result, the late 1980s and early 1990s were characterized by a "de facto convergence" of government policy approaches towards FDI (Noorbakhsh, Paloni, and Youssef, 2001).

The liberalization of FDI policy was both cause and effect of the marked increase in integration of the world economy in the 1990s which, in turn, reflected the transition of the ex-socialist to market economies after the "fall of the Wall", dramatic improvements in communication as a result of the digital/information revolution, changes in the nature of global production including the internationalization of supply chains and the ideological shift to open market economies, among other factors. Increasing economic integration, which includes policy liberalization, is reflected in dramatic increases in flows of FDI into developing countries during the late 1980s and the 1990s. Annual inflows to the developing countries grew by 250% during

---

[3] After a critical review of studies of trade liberalization, Stanley Fischer (2003, p. 15) concludes that "...openness to the global economy is a necessary, though not sufficient, condition of sustained growth."

the 1980s and over five-fold (520%) during the 1990s, reaching $22.9 billion in 1999. FDI inflows as a percentage of gross fixed capital formation in developing countries grew from 3.6% in 1990 to 14.3% by the decade's end. Last, stocks of FDI as a percentage of GDP doubled during the 1990s, increasing from 15.4% in 1989 to 30.2% in 1999 (UNCTAD, 2004).

This article reports a cross-sectional analysis of the determinants of liberalization of policy affecting inflows of FDI into 116 developing countries during the decade from 1992-2001. It makes use of a data base provided by UNCTAD (described below) that tracks liberalizing and restricting changes in eight categories of FDI policy by country over the ten year period. The changes were overwhelmingly liberalizing: 95% of the 1,086 regulatory changes in the sample countries either loosened regulatory restrictions or provided new promotions and guarantees to attract FDI; all but two of the countries included in this study were net liberalizers of FDI policy.

Liberalization of FDI policy

In their path-breaking study of capital account liberalization, Dennis Quinn and Carla Inclan (1997) note that, while there has been a good deal of research on the consequences of financial openness, its origins or determinants are much less well understood. That is true for both capital flows in general and FDI in particular. [4]

While there is a considerable literature dealing with the impact of tax concessions and other incentives to attract FDI (see Morisset and Pirnia, 2001 for a review), the literature

---

[4] See Eichengreen (2001) for a thorough review of capital account liberalization. It is important to note that portfolio flows and FDI are very different both phenomenologically and in terms of cause and effect. As a number of authors note (e.g. Eichengreen, 2001; Fischer, 2003; Prasad *et al.*, 2003) there is a good deal more controversy about the desirability and impacts of capital account liberalization (on growth and stability) than there is for current account or trade liberalization.

dealing with FDI policy is considerably more modest. Alvin Wint (1992), for example, reviews the liberalization of FDI regulation in ten developing countries and concludes that there can be a disconnect between formal liberalization and the actual implementation of the screening process. Stephen Golub (2003) presents a complex scheme summarizing liberalization of restrictions on inward FDI in OECD countries. Jacques Morisset and Olivier Neso (2002) review administrative barriers to inflows of FDI in 32 least developed countries (LDCs). A larger body of work examines the impact of administrative reform or liberalization of regulation on either inflows of FDI or the FDI decision process (Gastanaga, Nugent and Pashamova, 1998; Globerman and Shapiro, 2003; Loree and Guisinger, 1995; Sin and Leung, 2001; Taylor 2000; Trevino, Daniels, and Arbelaez, 2002).

There are few empirical analyses of the determinants of liberalization of laws and regulations affecting inflows of FDI. A study by the United Nations Centre on Transnational Corporations in 1991 looked at changes in FDI policies in 46 developed and developing countries over the years 1977-1987. It constructed a data base of changes in seven categories of regulation affecting FDI, including both restrictions and incentives. The study concluded that there was "[A]n unmistakable liberalization of foreign direct investment policies in all categories of nations" over the 1980s, with the largest number of policy changes per country occurring in the newly industrializing countries (UNCTC, 1991, p. 59). While the author argued that the recession of the early 1980s, the relative decline in the position of developing countries, the increased tightening of the market for loan finance to developing countries, and a generally increased climate of competition for FDI all contributed to the increase in liberalization, the empirical analysis focuses on the impact of liberalization on future flows of FDI rather than its determinants.

Discussing the globalization of financial markets, Benjamin Cohen (1996, p. 278) asks a very relevant question about the motivations for state behaviour: "Were states operating as classic rational unitary actors, single-mindedly competing within systemic constraints to maximize some objective measure of national interest? Or were other, more subtle forces at work to shape government preferences and perceptions?"

Cohen's question certainly applies to the widespread liberalization of FDI policy in developing countries during the 1990s. On the one hand, it is possible that liberalization reflects a "rational" policy making process, a decision that the benefits of increased flows of FDI are greater than the costs. As Geoffrey Garrett (2000, p. 943) argues, "...increasing costs of closure probably have been the major motivation for liberalization in the arena of foreign direct investment..."[5] Thus, one possibility is that policy makers in developing countries reacted independently to changed technological and economic conditions and decided that liberalization to promote increased inflows of FDI was in the national interest.

Every economic argument, however, is "two-handed". It is also possible that policy-makers in developing countries responded to other "subtle" (or not so subtle) forces shaping their preferences and perceptions. External forces rather than a drive for efficiency may have motivated the widespread liberalization of FDI policy in developing countries during the 1990s (Cohen 1996; Garrett, 2000). External forces could include both coercive pressures to adopt neoliberal economic policies and/or emulation of actions taken in other comparable countries, a process of diffusion. It is important to note that it is possible for these views to be complementary as well as competing. Policy makers can be influenced by actions taken in other states or external political pressure and still make "rational" decisions based on the perceived "national interest".

---

[5] Put differently, "[T]he case for liberalizing FDI is similar to the case for liberalizing trade: under the right conditions, freer FDI leads to a more efficient allocation of resources across economies and, where markets are not distorted, within a host economy in the arena of foreign direct investment" (UNCTAD, 2003, p. 104).

What motivates liberalization?

A "rational" decision process

FDI can contribute to economic growth and development. It can add to fixed capital formation and have a positive balance-of-payments impact without the risks of debt creation or the volatility associated with short term portfolio capital flows. It can bring technology, know-how, managerial skills, technology and access to markets. It can increase the efficiency of local firms and the competitiveness of local markets (Gastanaga, Nugent and Pashamova, 1998; Javorick, 2004; Noorbakhsh, Paloni and Youssef, 2001; UNCTAD, 1999).

However, as Theodore Moran (1998) notes, FDI can have both malign and benign effects. It may lower domestic savings, crowd out domestic producers, drain capital from the host country, introduce inappropriate technology and constrain managerial and technological spillovers to the host country. As noted above, a "rational" decision to liberalize FDI policy assumes that the benefits of increased flows of FDI will outweigh the costs. The question, then, is the conditions under which that assumption is likely to be true.

While FDI can bring a wide range of potential benefits, transfers or spillovers of management, skills, know-how, organizational capabilities and technology are of particular interest to developing countries. A number of studies have found that the probability of spillovers taking place is a function of the host country's absorptive capacity which, in turn, is a function of the level of economic development, the degree of education of the workforce and the extent of competition in the host economy (Blomstrom, 2002; Kokko and Blomstrom, 1995; Lim, 2001; UNCTAD, 1999). Thus, one would expect policy makers to be more likely to assume that increased flows of FDI are in the national interest – and thus be more likely to liberalize – in countries with higher levels of development and better educated labour forces.

FDI, however, can bring a number of benefits beyond spillovers or transfers. In many cases immediate effects such as increased investment or employment may be just as important. There is increasing recognition that TNCs can make a significant contribution to export capabilities and increased concern about export competitiveness in many developing countries (UNCTAD 2002).

At present, all developing countries maintain some form of application or approval process for FDI: no country offers an unlimited right of entry to foreign investors (UNCTAD, 2003). Furthermore, as noted above, developing countries' confidence in their ability to deal with foreign investors on favourable terms has increased markedly in the past two decades. Thus, policy makers may now believe that they can achieve their objectives vis-à-vis foreign investors through negotiation rather than regulation. As bargaining power is, at least in part, a function of market size, countries with larger markets may be more likely to believe that they can drive a bargain where the benefits of FDI are greater than the costs and thus be more likely to liberalize.

Coercion and emulation

More "subtle forces" in the form of external pressures could also be responsible for liberalization of FDI policy in developing countries. Neoliberalism – a belief in markets, privatization, deregulation and open economies which took hold in the United States and United Kingdom during the 1980s – may have been "imposed" on developing countries (altering policy makers' preferences) as a result of economic dependence on the United States or on international institutions such as the World Bank and IMF. Policy liberalization also could have resulted from a process of diffusion, with policy makers' perceptions and preferences altered by actions taken in other countries of interest such as those in the region or those regarded as competitors.

That said, distinguishing empirically between these two competing categories of explanation is difficult at best: "It is a common problem in the literature on contagion, financial and other wise, that the simultaneity of policy initiatives in different countries may reflect not the direct influence of events on one country on another countries but a tendency for decision makers to respond similarly to economic and political events not adequately controlled for in the analysis" (Eichengreen, 2001, p. 350). The conceptual problem is exacerbated by the limitations of cross-sectional analysis.

While this article will not test a diffusion hypothesis directly, the analysis includes two sets of explanatory variables. The first is consistent with a rational efficiency explanation for liberalization. It contains indicators of national characteristics that would lead policy makers to believe that their countries would benefit from increased flows of FDI, that liberalization of FDI policy – either a loosening of restrictions or an increase in incentives – reflects a judgment that a country will benefit from either more FDI or fewer restrictions on existing investment. The second set of indicators is consistent with an externally imposed motivation for liberalization, with the imposition of a neoliberal ideology through pressure from either the United States or international institutions. As will be discussed below, control variables are also included in the analysis.

The determinants of liberalization

This study reviews two sets of determinants of liberalization of FDI policy. The first assumes that liberalization reflects a "rational" judgment by policy makers that their country will benefit from either more FDI or fewer restrictions on existing investment, that there is "an opportunity cost of closure" in terms of lost efficiency. The second assumes that liberalization results from the external imposition of a neoliberal economic ideology. A number of control variables are also included in the analysis.

Opportunity costs of closure

- *Country size.* There are two reasons to believe that country size will be positively related to liberalization. First, as discussed above, developing countries in general have become more confident of their ability to maintain a positive benefit-cost ratio for FDI through negotiation with foreign investors. One clear conclusion of empirical research on the determinants of FDI is that variables related to market size dominate (Nunnenkamp and Spatz 2002). Thus, *ceteris paribus*, larger countries are likely to have greater bargaining power vis-à-vis investors and may be more likely to liberalize, substituting negotiation for regulation. Second, larger markets are more likely to attract market-seeking FDI, and market-seeking FDI is more likely to result in technological and managerial spillovers – by developing forward and backward linkages – than that which is strictly export oriented. (A possible counter argument is that the greater bargaining power of larger countries may allow them to maintain restrictions if so desired. However, given the general tendency towards deregulation and liberalization, that is unlikely to dominate the first two arguments.)
- *Level of development.* As noted above, there is a general consensus that one of the primary benefits of FDI – managerial and technological spillovers – are more likely to occur at higher levels of development as the absorptive capacity of the host country is higher and the "gap" between foreign investors and local firms lower. Furthermore, it is reasonable to argue that the wealthier developing countries should have more developed public sector capabilities and institutions and thus be able to obtain greater benefits from FDI and be more likely to liberalize. However, *ceteris paribus*, it is also possible that less developed countries recognize a greater need for FDI and thus will be more willing to liberalize restrictions and offer incentives or guarantees to attract TNC investment. On balance, the first two arguments should dominate and a country's level of development should be positively related to the propensity to liberalize.

- *Growth of GDP.* Policy makers in countries experiencing economic growth are more likely to believe that increased investment, including FDI, will have a positive impact. As important, distributional issues may be minimized in a rapidly growing economy and thus opposition to FDI may be muted. Thus, growth of GDP should be positively related to the tendency to liberalize.
- *Trade openness.* Recent studies have rejected the older argument that "tariff jumping" is an important explanator of FDI and that trade and FDI are substitutes. James Markusen (1997) concludes, at least for a relatively skilled, labour-scarce economy, that FDI and trade can be complementary to one another. He notes that trade and investment are not substitutes in that they often have opposite effects on important variables and that trade and investment considered jointly have different effects than either alone. That being the case, a country's openness to trade should be an indicator of policy makers' perceptions that linkages to the world economy have a positive effect on growth and development and that additional FDI would be beneficial. Thus, there should be a positive relationship between trade openness and the propensity to liberalize FDI policy.
- *Human resource capabilities.* As discussed above, higher levels of human resource capabilities are indicative of higher levels of absorptive capacity on the part of the host country and thus, a higher probability of significant spillovers of managerial techniques and technology to host country firms. Thus, in countries with higher levels of human resource capabilities, policy makers might believe that increased flows of FDI will be beneficial. It is also reasonable to argue that higher levels of human resource capability should be reflected in the public as well as the private sector and that countries with higher levels of capabilities should be more confident of their ability to negotiate with foreign investors. There should be a positive relationship between human resource capabilities and the propensity to liberalize FDI policy.

- *Democracy.* There have been a number of studies associating democracy with capital account liberalization (Eichengreen, 2001). While there are counter arguments, a democratic process may allow resolution of social conflicts that would otherwise lead to restrictions – that is, it should be more difficult to maintain restrictions on inflows of FDI which benefit a small minority of citizens (e.g. domestic industries threatened by foreign investors) in a democracy. That being said, trade and investment policy often benefits affected interest groups, even in large capitalist democracies. Thus, it is difficult to predict the effect of democracy on the propensity to liberalize FDI policy.

External factors affecting decision makers' perceptions

- *Dependence on the United States.* During the 1980s and 1990s, the Government of the United States strongly supported a neoliberal economic policy including deregulation, privatization and openness to the world economy. It is reasonable to argue that policy preferences of the dominant economic power have an impact on policy preferences in poorer countries, especially to the extent that those countries are dependent on the United States as an export market or for inflows of FDI. Thus, to the extent a developing country is dependent on the United States economically – in terms of its exports or inflows of FDI, for example – it might be more likely to liberalize FDI policy.
- *Dependence on international institutions.* Both the World Bank and IMF were strongly pro-market and pro-liberalization during the period of this study. The IMF in particular pressed an agenda of deregulation and liberalization on developing countries as conditions accompanying their loans. Thus, to the extent that a country is obligated to the IMF or the World Bank, it might be more likely to liberalize FDI policy.

Control factors

- *FDI penetration.* As discussed below, the data base used in this study is "left censored" in that the first year for which data are available is 1992. While there is every reason to believe that the "great wave" of both portfolio capital and direct investment liberalization in developing countries occurred during the 1990s (Brune et al., 2001; Eichengreen, 2001), it is necessary to control for the possibility of prior liberalization of FDI policy. Furthermore, the data used in this study measure changes in policy rather than the level of policy openness at any point in time; there is no indicator available of the level of FDI policy liberalization in each country at the start of the study. The level of FDI stocks normalized by GDP is used as a proxy for relative openness at the start of the period. The assumption is that, *ceteris paribus*, countries with higher levels of FDI penetration relative to the size of the economy were more likely to be more open to FDI in the past.

- *Growth of FDI.* Geoffrey Garrett (2000) argues that, at least in the case of portfolio capital, policy changes may lag "facts on the ground". Given the information revolution's impact on the relative ease of moving capital across borders and the difficulty that individual countries have in controlling portfolio flows, liberalization may be technologically determined, i.e. it may reflect the reality of increased flows into a country. While FDI represents a "tangible" cross-border flow and is thus much easier for a host country to control, it is still possible that liberalization is a *de jure* reflection of a *de facto* change. Thus, a relationship between the growth of FDI prior to the start of the period encompassed by the data and liberalization would be an indication of legitimization of *de facto* change.

- *Resource dependence.* Many of the major exporters of minerals and petroleum nationalized FDI at the well-head or mine in the late 1970s and then developed contractual arrangements for the involvement of TNCs during the 1980s. Thus, to the extent that a country is dependent on mineral exports (including petroleum) it should be less likely to report changes in FDI regulations during the 1990s.

The data

The UNCTAD database contains the *number* of annual changes in each of eight categories of national laws and regulations affecting inflows of FDI during the decade from 1992 to 2001. The categories, defined in appendix 1, are: foreign ownership; sectoral restrictions; approval procedures; operational conditions; foreign exchange; promotion including incentives; guarantees; and corporate regulations. There are two observations for each category-country-year: the number of more and of less favourable FDI policy changes (i.e. liberalizing and restricting). It should be clear that what is measured are *changes* in a country's openness to FDI rather than its level of openness at any point in time.

There are a number of reasons to be concerned about the accuracy and validity of the raw data as a comparative measure of change in FDI policy across countries. First, there is no information about the magnitude or extensiveness of change. Every liberalizing or restricting change is coded as one event regardless of whether it is a relatively major or relatively minor change. Second, there is no way to know if reporting is consistent across countries. It is possible, for example, that three changes in sectoral restrictions in a single year are reported as three separate changes by country A and only one by country B. As a result, there are serious questions about whether a continuous scale is an accurate or valid measure of the extent of regulatory change: does a score of "3" for a given country-category-year actually represent three times the "amount" of change of a score of "1"?

To attempt to minimize these problems and facilitate cross-sectional analysis, each category-country-year score was recoded to take one of three values: -1 if there were one or more restrictive changes; 0 if there was no change; and +1 if there were liberalizing changes. (Only 57 of the 1,086 regulatory changes in the sample countries were restrictive and there were only 13 instances in which a single country reported both liberalizing and restrictive changes in a single category in a single year. In these cases, the net score was used as a basis for coding.) While recoding results in some loss of information, it should allow for a more accurate representation of differences in changes in FDI policy across countries.

Country sample

The objective of this analysis is to identify the determinants of liberalization of FDI policy in developing countries. To that end, three categories of countries were dropped from the UNCTAD database: developed countries; those with cumulative inflows of FDI of under $50 million between 1991 and 2001; and those classified as tax havens by the OECD. That leaves a sample of 116 developing countries and economies in transition distributed as follows. (A country list is attached as appendix 2.)

Africa	32
Latin America and the Caribbean	22
Middle East	11
Central Asia	8
Asia and Pacific	24
Central and Eastern Europe	19

FDI policy changes

The decade encompassed by the data base (1992-2001) was one of widespread liberalization of FDI policy in the developing countries. Table 1 reports the total number of liberalizing ("more") and restrictive ("less") policy changes over the ten year period (the "raw" data) by category and region. Ninety-five per cent of the changes were liberalizing: 1,029 of the total of 1,086.

The most striking finding is that the single most important policy category over the decade was positive attempts to attract FDI in the form of promotion and incentives rather than a

Table 1. Changes in FDI policy, by region, 1991-2001
(Number)

Region	Africa	Latin American and the Caribbean	West Asia	Central Asia	South, East and Southeast Asia	Central and Eastern Europe	Total
Ownership							
more	2	9	11	1	18	6	47
less	0	0	0	0	1	3	4
Sectoral							
more	21	40	14	14	94	37	220
less	0	2	1	1	1	3	7
Approval							
more	9	6	8	5	18	6	52
less	0	0	1	0	2	1	4
Operational							
More	29	11	20	6	63	33	164
Less	0	0	1	1	1	2	5
Foreign exchange							
more	10	6	1	2	15	12	46
less	2	1	0	1	1	2	7
Promotion							
more	64	37	19	14	107	83	328
less	1	6	0	2	1	7	22
Guarantees							
more	13	33	24	8	27	21	126
less	0	0	0	0	1	0	1
Regulations							
more	6	5	3	4	20	8	46
less	0	2	0	0	1	4	7
Total							
more	154	147	100	54	362	206	1029
less	3	11	3	4	14	22	57

Source: UNCTAD database.
[a] Includes Pacific region not reported separately.

loosening of restrictions. Promotion and incentives account for almost one-third (31.5%) of the more liberalizing changes, loosening sectoral restrictions 21.4%, operational conditions 15.9%, and increasing guarantees 12.2%. These four categories account for over 80% of liberalizing FDI policy changes over the decade in question. Changes in regulations affecting ownership, approval procedures, foreign exchange and corporate regulations each accounted for only between four and five per cent of the total. I will return to the question of the importance of promotion and incentives below.

As noted above, given concerns about the accuracy and validity of the "raw" numbers of events, the data were recoded as −1, 0 and +1, reflecting de-liberalizing, no changes and liberalizing changes respectively in a given category-country-year observation. Table 2 contains the sum of the recoded country-year score (−1, 0, +1), by category. The distribution across categories parallels that of the raw data. Changes in promotion and other incentives designed to attract FDI account for just under one-third of total events. The regulatory categories with the highest reported frequency of change are sectoral restrictions, operational constraints and guarantees. Changes in ownership requirements, approval procedures, foreign exchange requirements and corporate regulations each account for only about five per cent of the total.

Table 2. Recoded events by category, 1992-2001

(Number and per cent)

Category	Number	Percentage
Ownership	40	5.7
Sectoral	143	20.3
Approval	38	5.4
Operations	102	14.5
Foreign exchange	37	5.3
Promotion	226	32.1
Guarantees	82	11.6
Regulations	36	5.1
Total	704	100.0

Source: UNCTAD database.

The number of countries actually liberalizing a given category of FDI policy, however, varies considerably. At one extreme, 75% of the countries in the sample enacted new laws or regulations providing promotions or incentives to attract FDI at least once during the decade in question. Fifty-eight per cent of countries liberalized sectoral restrictions, 51% provided guarantees and 47% liberalized operational conditions – again at least once during the decade. On the other hand, only 29% liberalized ownership regulations, 26% application procedures, 25% foreign exchange regulations and 22% corporate regulations.

It is important to reiterate that the data measure the number of laws or regulations enacted or changed over the period 1992-2001 rather than the level of a country's openness to FDI. Furthermore, data that would allow one to characterize FDI policy at the start of the period are not available. Thus, it is entirely possible that the relatively low number of countries liberalizing ownership regulations during the 1990s, for example, reflects earlier liberalization of this constraint. (An attempt is made to control for this problem statistically.)

Summing the recorded data across all eight categories and all ten years provides an indicator of the total net change in FDI policy for each country over the entire decade (Total). The value for Total in all but two of the countries in the sample was one or greater – that is 114 of the 116 countries in the sample were net liberalizers across all categories of FDI policy over the period from 1992-2001. (One country had a score of zero and another minus one.) The mean country recorded six (net) liberalizing changes in FDI policy over the decade and the median four. (Again, only five per cent of all of the changes recorded were deliberalizing.)

The distribution of Total across regions is shown in table 3. As can be seen, Asia – Pacific and Central and Eastern Europe (including Russia and Ukraine) stand out as having a higher per-country average than the mean of 6.1. Put differently, Asia –Pacific accounts for 31% of the country-year changes and 21% of the countries in the sample; the ratio of the percentage of events to percentage of countries is 148. It is 125 for Central and Eastern Europe.

China (32), India (27) and Viet Nam (27) were the three countries in the sample with the highest scores for Total. However, virtually all of the major Asian countries score well above the sample average. In the case of Central and Eastern Europe, while there are few outliers, many of these transitional countries had a higher than average tendency to liberalize FDI policy.

Table 3. Total by region, 1992-2001
(Number)

Region	Total	Number of economies	Total/ economy	Event/ economy ratio[a]
Africa	128	32	4.0	66
Latin America and the Caribbean	118	22	5.4	88
Mid-East	63	11	5.7	100
Central Asia	37	8	4.6	71
Asia-Pacific	219	24	9.1	148
Central and Eastern Europe	139	19	7.3	125
Total	704	116	6.1	

Source: UNCTAD database.
[a]   Percentage of changes in a region divided by percentage of economies in a region.

The number of net total regulatory changes by year is shown in figure 1. The trend over time shows two peaks over the decade, the years from 1993 to 1995 when the number of net regulatory changes ranged from 65 to 70 per year and 1998 to 2001 when the number of net changes ranged from 85 to 79. Analysis of trends over time is beyond the scope of this analysis.

That said, it is not unreasonable to assume that efforts to liberalize FDI policy in developing countries were limited and sporadic before the late 1980s as there is general consensus that the "great wave" of liberalization occurred during the 1990s. Given that assumption, several (admittedly speculative) inferences can be drawn from the data.

Figure 1. Total, by year, 1992-2001
(Number)

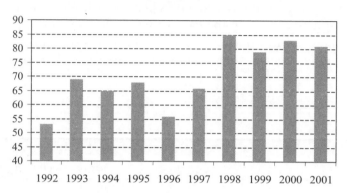

Source: UNCTAD database.

First, many developing countries attempted to attract FDI by *both* loosening policy restrictions and increasing investment incentives.   More specifically, two-thirds of the countries (78) recorded at least one liberalizing change in promotion and incentives and at least one of the other regulatory categories during the decade. While beyond the scope of a cross-sectional analysis, that is consistent with UNCTAD's "three generation" concept of investment promotion policy: liberalization of regulation in the first stage, followed by investment promotion in the second and specific targeting of investors in the third (UNCTAD, 2001).

Second, while virtually every country requires that foreign investments gain approval prior to entry, only 26% of the countries liberalized application procedures during the decade. Thus, even though many of the countries liberalized sectoral restrictions (58%) and operational conditions (48%), the vast majority did not make changes to their approval process.

Multivariate analysis

The approach taken in this preliminary analysis of the UNCTAD data base is cross-sectional. That is, policy changes for each country are summed over the ten years and the analysis examines the decade as a whole.

A correlation matrix of the eight regulatory categories is shown as table 4.[6] As can be seen, there is a very high degree of inter-correlation among the eight categories: the correlation coefficient is significant in all but three of the cells.[7] The relatively high correlation between promotion and operations (0.51) and sectoral (0.38) confirms the tendency of countries to attract FDI though both removing restrictions and offering positive incentives.

Table 4. Correlation matrix — regulatory categories

	own	sec	app	ops	forex	prom	guar	regs
own	1.0000							
sec	0.3721	1.0000						
	0.0000							
app	0.2685	0.2846	1.0000					
	0.0036	0.0020						
ops	0.3414	0.4085	0.4655	1.0000				
	0.0002	0.0000	0.0000					
forex	0.2719	0.4387	0.4466	0.5577	1.0000			
	0.0032	0.0000	0.0000	0.0000				
prom	0.2632	0.3771	0.2173	0.5066	0.4386	1.0000		
	0.0043	0.0000	0.0191	0.0000	0.0000			
guar	0.2209	0.3083	0.0771	0.1323	0.2747	0.3128	1.0000	
	0.0172	0.0008	0.4110	0.1568	0.0028	0.0006		
regs	0.3504	0.4483	0.2367	0.3732	0.5463	0.2005	0.2437	1.0000
	0.0001	0.0000	0.0105	0.0000	0.0000	0.0310	0.0084	

Source: author's calculations.
Note: N = 116.

---

[6] Stata 8.0 was used for all statistical analysis.
[7] China is a clear outlier as its score for Total is 32, compared with a median of 4. India and Viet Nam are also outliers as their scores for Total are each 27. The matrix is robust as the virtually all of the correlations remain significant even if these three countries are deleted.

As Cronbach's Alpha for an unweighted index of the eight variables (Total) is quite high at 0.76, it is productive to look at the regulatory categories in aggregate. For any given country, Total could range from –80 if it had a deliberalizing regulatory change in each of the eight categories in each of the ten years to +80: in practice, the minimum is –1 and the maximum 32. Total is interpreted as the sum of category-years in which there was a net liberalizing regulatory change. The sum of Total for all of the countries in the sample is 704, i.e., there were 704 of a possible 1,160 country-years in which a net liberalizing event took place.

Independent variables[8]

The independent and control variables are operationalized as follows:
- country size: GDP in current $US in1991; population in 1991;
- level of development (GDP/Cap): GDP per capita (GDP/ Capita) in current $US in 1991;
- growth in GDP (grGDP): growth in GDP during 1987-1991;
- trade openness (open): exports + imports/ GDP for 1991;
- human resource capabilities (sch): second level school enrollment ratio for 1991;
- democracy (dem);[9]
- dependence on the United States (ex-US): the proportion of a country's exports going to the United States in 1991;
- dependence on international institutions (IMF91): presence or absence of IMF obligations in 1991;
- FDI penetration (FDI/GDP): FDI stock/GDP for 1991;
- growth in FDI (grFDI): growth in stocks of FDI during 1987-1991;
- resource dependence (minexs): the percentage of exports accounted for by minerals (including petroleum) in 1991.

[8] Data sources include: IMF Financial Statistics; Penn World Tables; UNCTAD's FDI Data Base; World Bank Development Indicators; and the Polity IV Data File.

[9] Democracy is computed from the Democratic and Authoritarian scores for each country in the Polity IV file. Each ranges from 1 – 10 and, as is the convention, Authoritarian is subtracted from Democratic to compute a variable with a range of –10 to +10.

Unless otherwise noted, data for the independent variables were collected for 1991, immediately prior to the period encompassed by the database.

Table 5 contains pair-wise correlation coefficients for Total and each of the predictor and control variables. The strongest bivariate relationships are found between Total and country size (GDP), the measure of human resource capabilities (secondary school enrollment ratio) and the growth of FDI from 1986-1991. (GDP and per capita GDP are transformed logarithmically.) None of the other independent variable's coefficients with Total are significant.

Ordinary least squares (OLS) regression results are shown in table 6. Three points should be noted before the regression results are discussed. First, the range of the dependent variable is limited. In theory it could vary from -80 to $+80$; in practice it ranges from -1 to 32. However, as results are virtually identical if the bounded nature of the dependent variable is taken into account (Tobit), OLS is reported. Second, due to data limitations, the sample of countries used in multivariate analyses ranges from 64 to 79 of the 116 countries drawn from the UNCTAD database. (There are no missing values for any of the dependent variables, Total or FDI policy categories.) The deletions are not random as, at a minimum, all eight of the Central Asian countries and ten of the nineteen Eastern and Central European countries are not included in the analysis. Last, as tests indicate heteroskedasticity (Cook-Weisberg), results are reported for robust estimates using the Huber – White correction.

Model 1 contains four explanatory variables (lGDP, lGDP/ Cap, Sch and Open) and FDI/GDP as a control variable. A total of 79 countries are included in the analysis. The independent variables account for 63% of the variance of Total.[10] Market size (lGDP) is the single most important determinant of a

---

[10] As robust regression is used to correct for heteroskedasticity, adjusted r-squares are not available.

Table 5. Correlation matrix

	Total	lGDP	lGDP/Cap	open	sch	FDI/GDP	grFDI	grGDP	minexs	ex-US	dem
Total	1.0000										
lGDP	0.6277	1.0000									
	0.0000										
lGDP/Cap	-0.0086	0.3847	1.0000								
	0.9318	0.0001									
open	-0.0958	-0.1454	0.4509	1.0000							
	0.3803	0.1896	0.0000								
sch	0.2066	0.3153	0.6449	0.2678	1.0000						
	0.0319	0.0015	0.0000	0.0138							
FDI/GDP	-0.0891	0.0482	0.2871	0.6152	0.0868	1.0000					
	0.3830	0.6480	0.0055	0.0000	0.4027						
grFDI	0.3960	0.5715	0.3040	0.4734	0.1680	0.4768	1.0000				
	0.0001	0.0000	0.0038	0.0000	0.1095	0.0000					
grGDP	0.1670	0.1928	-0.0054	0.1857	-0.2913	0.2871	0.4196	1.0000			
	0.0871	0.0547	0.9575	0.0907	0.0028	0.0050	0.0000				
minexs	-0.0052	-0.0202	0.0265	-0.0540	-0.0112	0.0115	-0.1001	-0.1097	1.0000		
	0.9666	0.8721	0.8328	0.6875	0.9281	0.9273	0.4204	0.3808			
ex-US	-0.0595	0.1020	0.0849	0.0565	-0.0032	0.1460	0.2408	0.1198	-0.1558	1.0000	
	0.5863	0.3589	0.4452	0.6253	0.9769	0.1798	0.0264	0.2775	0.2153		
dem	0.1399	0.1959	0.1447	-0.0565	0.1636	0.0377	0.0960	-0.1494	0.0797	0.3311	1.0000
	0.1566	0.0642	0.1736	0.6254	0.1093	0.7285	0.3763	0.1485	0.5313	0.0029	

Source: author's calculations.

Table 6. Regressions on Total

Variable	Model 1	Model 2	Model 3	Model 4	Model 5	Model 6	Model 7
lGDP	3.141***	2.815***	2.740***	3.142***	2.929***	2.557***	3.563***
	(.442)	(.406)	(.443)	(.439)	(.430)	(.431)	(.672)
lGDP/Cap	-3.854***	-3.286**	-2.433**	-3.582**	-3.260**	-2.966**	-3.227**
	(.043)	(1.056)	(.885)	(1.102)	(1.072)	(1.218)	(1.021)
sch	.106***	.098***	.090***	.095***	.099***	.089***	.087***
	(.023)	(.022)	(.024)	(.022)	(.024)	(.024)	(.024)
open	.030**	.028**	.029**	.053**	.034**	.031**	.043**
	(.012)	(.010)	(.011)	(.020)	(.012)	(.012)	(.016)
FDI/GDP	-.027	-.030	-.049	-.020	-.085	-.036	-.024
	(.027)	(.025)	(.028)	(.030)	(.027)	(.025)	(.022)
china		12.508***	14.268***	12.161***	12.075***	14.028***	16.359***
		(2.533)	(2.519)	(2.493)	(2.074)	(2.726)	(2.950)
minexp			.021				
			(.019)				
IMF91				.002			
				(.005)			
ex-US					-2.216		
					(2.074)		
dem						.084	
						(.068)	
grFDI							-.000
							(.000)
constant	-46.223***	-42.147***	-46.450***	-49.695***	-44.792***	-38.311***	-59.846***
	(7.184)	(6.423)	(7.026)	(7.223)	(6.835)	(6.105)	(3.051)
F	24.51***	24.40***	23.62***	21.67***	20.72***	17.90***	22.10***
r-sq.	.627	.670	.747	.700	.687	.669	.692
N	79	79	64	73	74	70	77

Source: author's calculations.
*** p <= .001 ** p<= .01 * p<= .05
Standard errors are shown below the coefficient in parenthesis

country's overall propensity to liberalize, using *either* GDP or population as a measure it alone accounts for 39% of the variance of Total.[11] The secondary enrollment ratio as a proxy for human resource capabilities and trade openness are both highly significant and positive. GDP/Capita is significant and negative. The coefficient of the control variable (FDI/GDP) is not significant.

GDP/Capita (a proxy for the level of development) was not significantly correlated with Total on a univariate basis. Furthermore, in a regression containing population as a measure of country size and GDP/Capita, both are significant and positive, accounting for 47% of the variance in Total. However, once the secondary enrollment ratio is entered into this equation, GDP/Capita becomes negative and insignificant. As noted above, in the equation containing GDP as a proxy for country size, GDP/Capita is negative and significant.

It is difficult to interpret the role of the level of development in this analysis. It is not significant in itself (in a univariate regression equation) and it turns significant and negative in interaction with GDP as a measure of country size. However, if population is used as a proxy for country size, its coefficient is significant and positive. The coefficient becomes negative once the school enrollment ratio is introduced into the equation (the two variables are highly correlated). Thus, the most that can be said is that there is an indication that larger countries are more likely to liberalize if they are more developed (i.e. a higher GDP/Capita) but that effect is swamped by the proxy for human resource development.

Model 2 adds a dummy variable to control for China which is a clear outlier (Total = 32). As can be seen, aside from a slight increase in the variance explained (67%), the results are virtually identical to model 1. (The coefficient for China is significant and positive.) The OLS regressions are robust as

---

[11] Standardized coefficients (betas) allow a direct comparison: lGDP (.801); lGDP/Cap (-.673); sch (.443); open (.260); and FDI/GDP (-.110).

---

the coefficients are very similar when the three clear outliers (China, India and Viet Nam) are dropped from the equation. Multicollinearity does not appear to be a problem: the variable inflation factor (VIF) for each of the independent variables in models 1 and 2 is under three and the mean VIF two or less.

Models 3 through 7 add other independent variables to the base equation (model 2), mineral exports, IMF obligations, United States export dependence, democracy and growth of FDI. None are significant, even at the .10 level. It should be noted that the sample size varies for models 3 through 7 due to missing data. (The equation for growth in GDP is not reported.)

As noted above, due to missing data (independent variables), all of the ex-Soviet republics in Central Asia are dropped from the regressions, as are over half of the Central and Eastern European countries. However, data for GDP and per capita GDP are available for most of the Central and Eastern European countries and half of the Central Asian states. A regression including both of these variables as well as a dummy variable, coded one for a transitional or ex-socialist country, is of interest. The three independent variables account for 51% of the variance (adjusted r-squared) and the dummy variable is positive and significant. Thus, the economies in transition were more likely to liberalize, holding country size and level of development constant.

Regressions were also run for each of the four most important categories of FDI policy individually: operational constraints; sectoral limitations; promotion and incentives; and guarantees. In each case, market size (GDP) was the primary determinant of liberalization of FDI policy. There are some differences among the four, however (regression results are not reported). In the regression equation for operations, open (exports plus imports over GDP) was not statistically significant and both export dependence on the United States and the growth of FDI (over 1986 through 1991) were significant at the .05 level or better. The only difference observed for sectoral limitations is that open was not significant. The control variable for China was not significant for either promotion or guarantees. Export dependence on the United States was significant for promotion. Last, the set of independent variables explained only 24% of the variance of guarantees, and the only significant explanators were GDP, open and FDI/GDP, which was negative.

Discussion

The single most important determinant of liberalization of FDI policy during the 1990s (1992 through 2001) is market size, with a strong positive impact; either GDP or population explains 39% of the variance of Total. The larger a country the higher the value of Total – the measure of overall liberalization; larger countries reported a larger number of category-years in which net liberalization was positive.

This analysis cannot confirm the specific mechanism linking country size and liberalization of FDI policy. However, at a minimum it would appear reasonable to argue that countries with larger markets are more likely to believe that the net benefits from additional inflows of FDI are likely to be positive. As noted above, this could be a function of bargaining power, a perception on the part of policy makers that objectives can be achieved through negotiation rather than regulation. It may also reflect the fact that larger countries are more likely to attract market-seeking FDI, which may entail a greater likelihood of spillovers than that which is resource or export oriented.

Countries that were more open to trade before the start of the period were more likely to liberalize FDI during the decade in question. That appears reasonable from a number of perspectives. First, trade openness indicates a general predisposition to economic openness, a belief that growth and development are enhanced by linkages to world economy. As noted above, recent research indicates that trade and FDI can be complements rather than competitors. Thus, trade openness should be an indicator of a belief that FDI and TNCs are net contributors to growth and development. Second, trade openness may lead to a concern for export competitiveness and an appreciation of the roles that TNCs can play in generating export capabilities.

The importance of school enrollment ratios as a proxy for human resource capabilities reflects the fact that a country with a better educated work force is more likely to absorb potential spillovers of management and technology from TNCs and thus FDI is likely to be more highly valued. Thus, countries with higher levels of human resource capabilities are more likely to want to attract FDI through liberalization of regulation and/or offering incentives and guarantees. Furthermore, school enrollment ratios should proxy public as well as private sector capabilities, and countries with a more educated public sector workforce may have more confidence in their ability to deal with TNCs on favourable terms.

The coefficient for GDP/Capita is more difficult to interpret. As noted above, it is not significantly related to Total on a univariate basis and the direction and significance of its coefficient appears to be a function of interaction with other independent variables. The most that can be said is that the fact that GDP/Capita is significant in an equation with population as a measure of country size does not contradict a hypothesis that spillovers are more likely at higher levels of development and FDI is thus seen as more attractive.

It is important to note that the data used in this study reflect changes rather than levels of openness, and the earliest year for which data are available is 1992. While FDI/GDP in 1991 is used to attempt to control for the previous level of FDI, it is entirely possible that at least some of the wealthier countries liberalized before 1992. However, even when the wealthier countries are dropped from the regression, using GDP to proxy market size, the relationship between Total and per capita GDP is negative and significant. Further research is necessary to confirm and explain this finding.

None of the other independent variables were significant predictors of Total. However, export dependence on the United

States was significant in the equations for operational constraints and promotions and incentives. Thus, it is possible that external pressure in the form of coercion from the United States to adopt neoliberal economic policies played a role in at least these two aspects of FDI policy change. Further research is needed to fully explore this possibility.

Conclusions

Changes in FDI policy over the decade encompassed by this study were overwhelmingly liberalizing: 95% of the 1,086 individual policy changes either lessened restrictions on inflows of FDI or provided additional promotions and incentives to attract increased flows. All but two of the countries (Kazakhstan and Kenya) out of the 116 studied were net liberalizers.

Two alternative explanations for the liberalization of FDI policy were discussed. The first argues that liberalization reflects a "rational" decision on the part of host country policy makers, a response to changed technological and economic conditions or the increasing "costs of closure" for FDI. In this view, liberalization reflects a belief that lower barriers and increased flows of FDI are in the national interest. The second argues that liberalization was a response to external factors, specifically, the spread of neoliberal ideology possibly through pressure from either the United States or international financial institutions.

The results of this analysis are certainly consistent with the efficiency or "costs of closure" argument. Liberalization of FDI policy is a function of market size, trade openness and human resource capabilities, controlling for FDI penetration. As noted, the role of the level of economic development (GDP/ Capita) is difficult to interpret. It appears that policy makers in larger countries with higher levels of human resource capabilities where the benefits of FDI could reasonably be expected to outweigh the costs were interested in attracting more FDI, either through liberalization of regulation or offering new incentives and guarantees.

The analysis provides only limited support for an external pressure explanation of liberalization. While none of the variables operationalizing the external pressure explanation were significant as explanators of Total, it should be noted that export dependence on the United States was significant in the equations for operational constraints and promotion. That at least raises the possibility that external pressure plays a role in FDI policy liberalization, at least for these two categories of policy. However, given the limitations of cross-sectional analysis the most that can be said for the external pressure argument is the old Scottish verdict of "not proven".

While there are other possible modes of diffusion of neoliberal ideology (such as emulation of the actions of regional neighbors or competitors), it is not possible to test a diffusion hypothesis through cross-sectional analysis. Those issues must be left for further research.

Four policy categories accounted for over 80% of the changes: promotion and incentives (31.5%); sectoral restrictions (21.4%); operational conditions (15.9%); and guarantees (12.2%). The most important policy change in terms of frequency of occurrence was increased incentives offered to investors, e.g. tax reductions, training, infrastructure provisions. Seventy-five per cent of the countries in the sample offered new promotions and/or incentives at least once during the period 1992 to 2001. Furthermore, countries that offered increased promotion were also likely to reduce operational barriers and sector restrictions limiting inflows of FDI; the simple correlation between promotion and operations is .51 and that for sectoral .38 (table 4).[12]

That raises an important policy question: are reducing operational restrictions and/or sectoral limitations a substitute

---

[12] A factor analysis not separately reported confirms the relationship between promotion and operations, which are the only two variables "loading" on the second of three factors which together account for about half of the variance of the eight categories of FDI policy considered in this study.

for increasing promotions and incentives? As this analysis looks at the determinants rather than the effects of liberalization, nothing can be said about the relative impact of reducing restrictions versus increasing incentives as a means of attracting further flows of FDI. However, the results do raise the possibility that the two are seen, at least to some extent, as substitutes by policy makers. If that is the case, given that many studies of the impact of promotions and incentives conclude that it is a zero-sum game across host countries, policy makers might be encouraged to consider liberalizing restrictions rather than offering increased incentives as a means of attracting increased inflows of FDI. Again, it is important to note that no conclusions can be drawn about the substitutability of liberalization of restrictions and promotions based on the data and analysis in this study. The question, however, is certainly of interest.

Further research is required to answer a number of the questions raised in this analysis. Longitudinal analysis, specifically some form of cross-sectional time-series analysis, is needed to deal more rigorously with both the question of the relative importance of external pressure (coercion) and diffusion as explanations of policy liberalization. It would also be of interest to use the data to pursue studies of the impact of liberalization on future flows of FDI. ■

References

Blomstrom, Magnus (2002). "The economics of international investment incentives", in *International Investment Incentives* (Paris: OECD), pp. 165-183.

Brune, Nancy, Geoffrey Garrett, Alexandra Guisinger and Jason Sorens (2001). "The political economy of captial account liberalization". (New Haven: Yale University), mimeo.

Cohen, Benjamin J. (1996). "Phoenix risen: the resurrection of global finance", *World Politics,* 48 (2), pp. 268-296.

Eichengreen, Barry (2001). "Capital account liberalization: what do cross-country studies tell us?", *The World Bank Economic Review*, 15 (3), pp. 341-365.

Fischer, Stanley (2003). "Globalization and its challenges: Ely Lecture presented at the American Economic Association", mimeo.

Garrett, Geoffrey (2000). "The causes of globalization", *Comparative Political Studies,* 33 (6/7), pp. 941-991.

Gastanaga, Victor M., Jeffrey B. Nugent and Bistra Pashamova (1998). "Host country reforms and FDI inflows: how much difference do they make?" *World Development,* 26 (7), pp. 1299-1314.

Globerman, Steven and Daniel Shapiro (2003). "Governance infrastructure and U.S. foreign direct investment", *Journal of International Business Studies,* 34, pp. 19-39.

Golub, Stephen S. (2003). "Measures of restrictions on inward foreign direct investment for OECD countries", *OECD Economic Studies,* 36, pp. 88-122.

Gore, Charles (2000). "The rise and fall of the Washington Consensus as a paradigm for developing countries", *World Development,* 28 (5), pp.789-804.

International Monetary Fund (2001). *World Economic Outlook* (Washington: International Monetary Fund).

Javorick, Beata Smarzynska (2004). "Does foreign direct investment increase the productivity of domestic firms: in search of spillovers through backward linkages", *American Economic Review,* 94 (3), pp. 605-627.

Kokko, Ari, and Magnus Blomstrom (1995). "Policies to encourage inflows of technology through foreign multinationals", *World Development,* 23 (3), pp. 459-468.

Lim, Ewe-Ghee (2001). "Determinants of, and the relation between, foreign direct investment and growth: a summary of the recent literature" (Washington: International Monetary Fund), mimeo.

Loree, David W. and Stephen E. Guisinger (1995). "Policy and non-policy determinants of U.S. Equity foreign direct investment", *Journal of International Business Studies,* 26 (2), pp. 281-300.

Markusen, James R. (1997). "Trade versus investment liberalization" (Cambridge: National Bureau of Economic Research), mimeo.

Millner, Helen V. (1999). "The political economy of international trade", *Annual Review of Political Science,* 2, pp. 91-114.

Moran, Theodore H. (1998). *Foreign Direct Investment and Development: The New Policy Agenda for Developing Countries and Countries in Transition* (Washington: Institute for International Economics).

Morisset, Jacques and Olivier Lumenga Neso (2002). "Administrative barriers to foreign investment in developing countries", *Transnational Corporations,* 11 (2), pp. 99-120.

Morisset, Jaques and Neda Pirnia (2001). "How tax policy and incentives affect foreign direct investment: a review" in, *Using Tax Incentives to Compete for Foreign Investment: Are They Worth the Costs?* eds. L. T. J. Wells, N. J. Allen, J. Morisset and N. Pirnia. (Washington: Foreign Investment Advisory Service), pp. 69-108.

Noorbakhsh, Farhad, Alberto Paloni and Ali Youssef (2001). "Human captial and FDI flows to developing countries: new empirical evidence", *World Development,* 29 (9), pp.1593-1610.

Nunnenkamp, Peter and Julius Spatz (2002). "Determinants of FDI in developing countries: has globalization changed the rules of the game?", *Transnational Corporations,* 11 (1), pp. 1-34.

Prasad, Eswar, Kenneth Rogoff, Shang-Jin Wei and M. Ayhan Kose (2003). "Effects of financial globalization on developing countries: some empirical evidence" (Washington, D.C., International Monetary Fund), mimeo.

Quinn, Dennis P. and Carla Inclan (1997). "The origins of financial openness: a study of current and captial account liberalization", *American Journal of Political Science*, 41 (3), pp.771-813.

Sin, Chor-Yiu and Wing-Fai Leung (2001). "Impacts of FDI liberalization on investment inflows", *Applied Economic Letters*, 8, pp. 253-256.

Taylor, Christopher T. (2000). "The impact of host government policy on U.S. multinational investment decisions", *World Economy,* 23 (5) pp. 635-647.

Trevino, Len J., John D. Daniels and Harvey Arbelaez (2002). "Market reform and FDI in Latin America: an empirical investigation", *Transnational Corporations*, 11 (1), pp. 30-48.

United Nations Conference on Trade and Development (UNCTAD) (1994). *World Investment Report 1993:Transnational Corporations and Integrated International Production* (New York: United Nations).

_____ (1999). *World Investment Report 1999: Foreign Direct Investment and the Challenge of Development* (New York and Geneva: United Nations).

_____ (2001). *World Investment Report 2001: Promoting Linkages* (New York and Geneva: United Nations).

_____ (2002). *World Investment Report 2002:Transtional Corporations and export Competitiveness* (New York and Geneva: United Nations).

_____ (2003). *World Investment Report 2003: FDI Policies for Development: National and International Perspectives* (New York and Geneva: United Nations).

_____ (2004). *Foreign direct investment data base* UNCTAD [cited 12 February 2004]. Available from http://www.unctad.org/Templates/Page.asp?intItemID=1890&lang=1.

United Nations Centre on Transnational Corporations (UNCTC) (1991). *Government Policies and Foreign Direct Investment* (New York: United Nations).

Williamson, John (2000). "What should the World Bank think about the Washington Consensus ", *The World Bank Research Observer,* 15 (2), pp. 251-64.

Wint, Alvin G. (1992). "Liberalizing foreign direct investment regimes: the vestigial screen", *World Development,* 20 (10), pp.1515-1529.

World Bank (1991). *World Development Report 1991: The Challenge of Development* (New York: Oxford University Press).

Appendix I
Category definitions

Incentives (promotional): measures providing incentives, fiscal and/or financial, creating special zones with facilities for FDI operations, establishing or reinforcing national institutions entrusted with the promotion of foreign investment, and setting up permanent or ad hoc councils that include foreign investors in their membership and offer advice to governments. Foreign ownership: allowing foreign investors to own companies or shares, properties (moveable or otherwise) and assets.

Approval procedures: introducing, streamlining or lifting of procedure for approval, authorization, admission and/or establishment of FDI and foreign investors (companies, branches, subsidiaries). Notice requirements are also included here.

Operational conditions: introducing, easing or lifting of performance requirements imposed on FDI and/or foreign investors, post establishment treatment, discrimination, internal administrative encumbrances etc.

Guarantees (protection): through internal and international mechanisms, in areas of intellectual property rights laws, dispute settlement, ownership and other proprietary rights and interests, and protection from subsequent changes to laws and regulations adversely affecting the interests of foreign investors. Movement of capital, including guarantees to repatriation and transfer of capital, income, profits and royalties.

Sectoral liberalization: access for the first time to an industry or further liberalization of various sectors and sub-sectors: *services*, including, financial, banking and telecommunications; *manufacturing;* and *natural resources*, including energy mining and hydrocarbon.

Corporate regulation: corporate governance, stock exchange, financial markets laws.

Foreign exchange: controls over exchange, including permission to possess other currencies, and the amounts thereof.

Appendix 2 – list of economies*

Africa	Latin America and the Caribbean	Middle East	Central Asia	Asia and Pacific	Central and Eastern Europe
Algeria	Argentina	Iran, Islamic Republic of	Armenia	Fiji	Bangladesh
Egypt	Bolivia	Jordan	Azerbajan	Guam	Brunei Darussalam
Morocco	Brazil	Kuwait	Georgia	Papua New Guinea	Cambodia
Sudan	Chile	Lebanon	Kazakhstan		China
Tunisia	Colombia	Oman	Kyrgyzstan	China	Hong Kong,
Angola	Costa Rica	Qatar	Tajikistan		India
Botswana	Dominican Republic	Saudi Arabia	Turkmenistan		Indonesia
Burkina Faso	Ecuador	Syrian Arab Republic	Uzbekistán		Korea, Democratic People's Republic of
Cameroon	El Salvador	Turkey	Albania		Korea, Republic of
Congo	Guatemala	United Arab Emirates	Belarus		Lao People's Democratic Republic
Cote d'Ivoire	Guyana	Yemen	Bosnia and Herzegovina		Malaysia
Eritrea	Honduras		Bulgaria		Mongolia
Ethiopia	Mexico		Croatia		Myanmar
Ghana	Nicaragua		Czech Republic		Nepal
Guinea	Paraguay		Estonia		Pakistan
Kenya	Peru		Hingary		Philippines
Madagascar	Uruguay		Latvia		Singapore
Malawi	Venezuela		Lithuania		Sri Lanka
Mali	Barbados		Macedonia, the Former Yugoslavia Republic of		Taiwan Province of China
Mauritania	Cuba		Moldova, Republic of		Thailand
Mauritius	Jamaica		Poland		Viet Nam
Mozambique	Trinidad and Tobago		Romania		
Namibia			Russian Federation		
Níger			Serbia and Montenegro		
Nigeria			Slovakia		
Senegal			Slovenia		
South Africa			Ukraine		
Swaziland					
Tanzania, United Republic of					
Uganda					
Zambia					
Zimbabwe					

Source: UNCTAD database.

* Economies are grouped by region.

FDI and inter-firm linkages:
exploring the black box of the Investment
Development Path

Joanna Scott-Kennel and Peter Enderwick*

The Investment Development Path purports that foreign direct investment acts as a catalyst for economic development in a host country. In this article we conduct a theoretical investigation of the *black box* of the Investment Development Path – specifically, the mechanisms by which inward foreign direct investment prompts domestic firms to augment their ownership-specific advantages. Using the tenets of the eclectic paradigm, we explore the relationships between the entry of transnational corporations, resource exchange via non-equity, inter-firm linkages, ownership-advantage augmentation, and a host country's progression through the stages of the Investment Development Path. We conclude that the contribution of inward direct investment to a country's economic development is positively related to the degree of linkage intensity at the firm level.

Keywords: foreign direct investment, inter-firm linkages, economic development

Introduction

There is growing interest among researchers and governments in the role of transnational corporations (TNCs) as agents of host country economic development (Blomstrom, 1991; Dunning and Narula, 1996). There is also a recognition that economic globalization, the importance of knowledge-based assets and the subsequent growth of alliance capitalism have

* The authors are Senior Lecturer in International Business at the Victoria University of Wellington, New Zealand and Professor of International Business at Auckland University of Technology, Auckland, New Zealand. The authors would like to thank three anonymous referees. for their comments. Contact: Joanna.Scott-Kennel@vuw.ac.nz.

not only fundamentally affected the way in which the assets and activities of TNCs are organized and undertaken, but also their impact on host economies (Cantwell and Narula, 2001; Dunning, 2001; Lundan and Hagedoorn, 2001; Narula and Dunning, 2000; Teece, 1992).

A widely used framework for looking at the relationships between inward foreign direct investment (FDI) by TNCs, outward FDI by domestic firms and economic development by the host country is the Investment Development Path (IDP) (Dunning, 1981). While much of the analysis of these relationships is conducted at a macro- (Dunning and Narula, 1996) or meso-level (Ozawa, 1996), the central idea of the IDP – that foreign TNCs might help indigenous firms to upgrade their capabilities – is firmly grounded at the micro or firm-specific level (Dunning, 1988). However, research on the IDP does not explore, in any detail, the mechanisms by which inward FDI prompts domestic host country firms to upgrade their own ownership (O) – advantages — and ultimately become outward investors themselves. We argue that these micro-level resource and capability transmission mechanisms constitute the *black box* of the IDP.

Thus, the purpose of this article is to illuminate the black box of the IDP – that is, to better understand the process of upgrading of resources and capabilities at the level of the firm as a result of foreign affiliate and domestic firm interaction. Specifically, we conduct a theoretical investigation of the types of non-equity resource transmission mechanisms (inter-firm linkages), and how these influence the ownership-location-internalization (OLI) configuration of a host economy and the subsequent progression through the stages of the IDP.

Literature review

The IDP and OLI frameworks

A principal contribution of the IDP to our understanding of a host country's development trajectory at the firm level is its recognition of the important relationship between inward FDI, the gradual development of competitive resources or O-advantages within indigenous firms, and eventual outward FDI. The framework purports that inward FDI plays an important role in fostering the capabilities that ultimately enable indigenous firms to undertake outward FDI. Given favourable receptor conditions, inward FDI provides the impetus for the upgrading of indigenous O-advantages through the introduction of new technologies, critical skills and knowledge, competition effects, and linkages with domestic enterprises. Thus, the IDP provides a dynamic framework within which to examine the relationship between a country's stage of economic development and the extent of inward and outward FDI activity, where government policy acts as a catalyst to change (Dunning and Narula, 1996; Durán and Ubeda, 2001; Ozawa and Castello, 2001).

The IDP suggests that a country may progress through five stages of economic development relative to the rest of the world (Dunning, 1981; 1986; Dunning and Narula, 1996). These stages are identified by the country's net outward direct investment (NOI) position (the stock of outward FDI less the stock of inward FDI) and level of economic development (proxied by GDP or GNP per capita). The relative position of countries on the IDP trajectory can be explained by the OLI paradigm: the extent and nature of O-advantages and resources of both foreign affiliates and indigenous firms; the location-specific (L) advantages available to all firms in the specific country, region or locality; and the extent to which the O-advantages of both foreign and indigenous firms, in conjunction with home and host country L-advantages, are utilized via cross-border internalization (I-advantages) (Dunning, 1993; Narula, 1996). The OLI elements will, in turn, be influenced by a country's economic structure and the development strategy and macro-organizational policies of government (Dunning and Narula, 1996). As the OLI configuration relative to other countries changes, so too does the country's NOI position and its stage of economic development.

The first stage of the IDP is characterized by a negative NOI, limited inward FDI and no outward investment. The country has very few L-advantages to attract inward FDI, and even if these exist, local infrastructure and O-advantages of domestic firms are insufficient to support inward, or outward, FDI. Economic development is at an early stage. In the second stage, L-advantages become more favourable in response to changes to government policy, and the NOI position becomes more negative as inward FDI increases.

In the third stage, competition in the domestic market rises as O-advantages of the inward investors diffuse through to local industry, and initial cost competitiveness advantages are lost. Low cost-seeking inward FDI is gradually replaced by market-seeking investment (Barry *et al.*, 2003). As local L- and O-advantages become more sophisticated, outward FDI by domestic firms emerges, thus improving both the NOI position and level of economic development. The mutually reinforcing relationship between a host country's economic development and NOI position has been empirically tested by Dunning (1980) and Narula (1996). It involves a process of micro-level development of O-specific advantages by domestic firms, which enables them to undertake outward FDI activity. This further enhances local firm capability and O-specific advantage. Coupled with improvements in L-advantages brought about by government policy conducive to host industry development, this is expected to lead to a higher level of economic development (GDP/GNP) over time.

Stage 4 has traditionally been demarcated by a shift to a positive NOI position, as outward FDI stock exceeds inward FDI stock (Dunning, 1981, 1986). However, a recent study found discrepancies between the level of economic development (as measured by GDP per capita) and the NOI position, prompting a redefinition of the fourth stage (Durán and Ubeda, 2001). The authors suggest that measures of economic structure other than GDP per capita should be jointly considered as proxies of a country's competitiveness. The reason is that Stage 4 countries have a developed country profile in terms of GDP per capita, level of structural development and economic and social infrastructure, they attract asset and market-seeking investment and engage in outward FDI to gain strategic assets and lower-cost labour – but some still exhibit low outward FDI intensities that sustain a negative NOI position (e.g. New Zealand (Akoorie,

1996), Ireland (Barry *et al.*, 2003)). The authors argue that a negative NOI may be attributed to a smaller endowment (and generation) of knowledge- or technologically-intensive intangible assets (Durán and Ubeda, 2001, 2003.)[1] They conclude that the distinguishing feature of Stage 4 countries is not necessarily a positive NOI position, but an exponential growth function of outward FDI stocks.

Stage 5 of the IDP is characterized by a NOI position that fluctuates around zero as both stocks of inward and outward FDI become balanced and reciprocal cross-haul investment between countries occurs (Dunning and Narula, 1996). Juan Durán and Fernando Ubeda (2001) also observe that this stage is difficult to test empirically and that a NOI fluctuating around zero is also characteristic of a country with negligible inward and outward FDI (i.e. stage 1).

Established stocks of inward FDI, strong growth in outward FDI and, in most instances, a positive NOI position, are the distinctive features of countries in Stages 4 and 5. Research suggests that for these to be achieved, a host country needs both an accumulation of knowledge intensive assets embodied in domestic firms and favourable L-advantages relative to competing locations. Durán and Ubeda (2001) find that Stage 4 countries that fail to make the progression to Stage 5 have similar levels of inward investment but not outward investment as the latter is inhibited by insufficient local development of knowledge-intensive O-advantages. Peter Buckley and Francisco Castro (1998) find that host government policy, as well as external political events, can shape a country's trajectory by affecting the attractiveness of the country's L-advantages to inward FDI. The development of local O-advantages and L-advantages can be mutually reinforcing. For example, clusters or agglomerations of knowledge-intensive firms contribute to the attractiveness of a specific locality to

---

[1] However, Belkan (2001), in a study of the Austrian IDP, argues that a low or negative NOI may not be a sign of weakness of the O-advantages of host country firms, but strength of host country L-advantages which serve to attract more inward FDI.

inward FDI from both later stage countries seeking strategic acquisitions and alliances (Cantwell and Iammarino, 2000; Dunning, 2000) and from earlier stage countries seeking to address asset deficiencies (Chen and Chen, 1998). One advantage may also mask a decline in the other: for example, improvements in the NOI position may not necessarily signal growing local capabilities to undertake outward FDI – it has also been interpreted as the influence of declining L-advantages on stocks of inward FDI (Duran and Ubeda, 2003; Castro, 2004).

The literature reveals that different configurations of O, L and I play a particularly important role in advancing a host economy through the different stages of the IDP. In earlier stages, L-advantages, including appropriate facilitative government policy and basic infrastructure, are important. Continued progression through the stages is driven by the development of O-advantages in domestic firms and the introduction of foreign O-advantages by affiliates. In particular, the development or the introduction of internationally mobile, created assets (i.e. technology and knowledge) appear to be an important accelerator of both outward FDI and the shift to Stages 4 and 5. The development of such assets relies on a mutually reinforcing interaction between the O-advantages associated with inward FDI and foreign affiliates, and those of domestic firms – which are, in turn, reliant on the local political, economic and structural environment (L-advantages).

Internalization strategy and augmentation of O-advantages

Traditional approaches to business strategy purport that TNCs benefit from internalizing transactions within the firm hierarchy, thus creating I-advantages by avoiding or exploiting market failure across national borders (Rugman, 1980; Buckley and Casson, 1985). These approaches infer that O-advantages are created internally in the home market and then transferred to affiliates that exploit these advantages offshore, taking advantage of foreign L-advantages to build further on firm competences. Under this scenario, affiliates are more likely to absorb local competence via acquisition rather than engaging in linkages with domestic firms.

However, more recent approaches, including the intangible asset model (Buckley and Cassson, 1976, 1998), the knowledge model (Kogut and Zander, 1993), and the centres of excellence model (Holm and Pedersen, 2000) propose that the process of O-advantage augmentation casts a much wider net than home country development. Increasingly important is the development of affiliate-specific advantages in a host economy (Rugman and Verbeke, 2001) and asset augmentation (rather than asset exploitation or acquisition). These strategies support the notion that firms undertake FDI to tap into skills, knowledge and competences contained within agglomerations of highly innovative firms and industries (Kuemmerle, 1996; Chen and Chen, 1998; Dunning and Lundan, 1998; Ostry and Gestrin, 1993). These approaches focus on exploiting value creating activities and resources from both internal and external networks (Ghoshal and Barlett, 1990; Griffith and Harvey, 2001).

Exploiting and augmenting resources and assets beyond the boundaries of the firm is not a new idea – to which the extensive literature on strategic alliances, networks and clusters is testimony (e.g. Enright, 2000; Lundan, 2002; Håkansson and Johanson, 1993; Ivarsson, 1999). This literature suggests that, where the value of external relationships is perceived to be higher than what may be achieved under the full internalization of O-advantages, a firm may choose to externalize certain firm-specific assets, resources and knowledge via linkages with external firms. Thus, externalization via linkages suggests a means by which TNC activity might contribute to the upgrading of indigenous firms through knowledge and technology spillovers (Narula and Sadowski, 2002; Cantwell and Piscitello, 2002).

Researchers have sought to incorporate more sophisticated elements of corporate strategy and structural complexity, such as alliances and networks, into the eclectic paradigm (Dunning, 1995; 1997; 2001; Madhok and Phene, 2001; Guisinger, 2001; Cantwell and Narula, 2001; Lundan and Hagedoorn, 2001; Scott-Kennel and Enderwick, 2004). For example, Kurt Pedersen (2003) offers useful insights as to how the eclectic paradigm might be extended to include non-equity relationships formed through networks and alliances. He concludes by suggesting that either O-advantages might be split up into two groups: those possessed exclusively by a firm and those shared with other firms; or that firms might trade-off the internalization dimension in favour of cooperative agreements. In other words, a decrease in I-advantages may enable an increase in O-advantages via access to local capabilities and competences.

However, despite the potential of inter-firm linkages to promote host country economic development, inadequate consideration is given to the implications of the formation of non-equity relationships on host country firm development within the context of the IDP/OLI literature (Cantwell and Narula, 2001). Specifically, the mechanisms by which resource diffusion or transfer might occur via foreign affiliate – domestic firm linkages have not been linked explicitly to these frameworks.

Industry spillovers and inter-firm linkages

Empirical research from the host country perspective offers insight into the impact of inward FDI on domestic firms. The general consensus of this research is that FDI offers an additional channel for the introduction of technology, innovation, new ideas, different organizational practices and new skills to a host country (Dunning, 1993). However, findings on the impact of these resources at the industry level are mixed. Some find the entry of FDI is associated with higher total factor or labour productivity (Kokko *et al.*, 1996; Barrell and Pain, 1997; Sadik and Bolbol, 2001), the creation of spillovers to local industry (Coe *et al.*, 1997) and increased exports by domestic firms (Aitken *et al.*, 1997), while others find limited indirect effects from FDI (Narula and Marin, 2003) or that spillovers are limited to firms with foreign ownership (Khawar, 2003; Aitken and Harrison, 1999).

Many researchers find that the degree to which FDI influences the upgrading of domestic firms depends on the extent of interaction between foreign and domestic firms and the existing level of host-country economic development. Luis De Mello (1997) finds that the greater the local value-added content of foreign affiliates in a host country's production and the more productivity spillovers occur, the greater the expected impact. Beneficial impacts from affiliate activities are more likely to occur when the host country has sufficiently developed local L- and O-advantages, including technology and absorptive capacity (Kokko, 1994; Görg and Strobl, 2003), human capital (Borensztein *et al.*, 1998; Engelbrecht, 1997), economic stability and open markets (Bengoa and Sanchez-Robles, 2003; Zhang, 2001) and domestic firm capabilities (Rodriguez-Clare, 1996; Blomstrom and Kokko, 1998). It is evident from these studies that a certain degree of local competence and absorptive capacity is required for the benefits of linkages and spillovers from affiliate activities to be realized.

Other researchers have looked at specific types of linkages at the firm level. A review of this research offers useful insights into the potential of non-equity inter-firm linkages to act as resource transmission mechanisms. From the literature we are able to identify two main types of linkages according to their potential for resource diffusion or transfer – indirect and direct (UNCTAD, 2001).

Indirect linkages occur as a result of the close proximity or agglomeration of firms within a locality. They do not involve inter-firm transactions or resource transfer; but externalities in the form of technology, knowledge and productivity spillovers that may occur through demonstration effects, competitive effects or worker mobility. Demonstration effects occur as domestic firms observe and emulate the activities of affiliates, enabling them to improve their efficiency (Bengoa and Sanchez-Robles, 2003; Zhang 2001). Competitive effects occur typically among firms that compete in the same industry and/or for the same customers. Competitive pressure from the affiliates' activities may either encourage better performance of domestic firms, or lead to crowding out of domestic competitors, depending on the level of existing capability (Markusen and Venables, 1999). The agglomeration of firms or the presence of TNCs may also increase overall levels of productivity (see above) or lead to the entry of indigenous firms into the industry (Görg and Strobl, 2002). Worker mobility occurs when former employees leave to set up their own businesses – taking with them knowledge about the affiliates' activities, capabilities and resources, in addition to the benefits of training and skill development they have received on the job (Buckley, 2004).

Direct linkages, in contrast, are characterized by inter-firm relationships where there is a direct transfer of resources, and include transactional relationships, such as backward (buy) and forward (supply) linkages with domestic suppliers and customers, contractual linkages with domestic franchisees or licensees, and collaborative or alliance relationships with domestic partners.

Much of the literature focuses on the extent to which affiliates source inputs locally (such as raw materials, components, finished goods, transportation or professional services) (McAleese and McDonald, 1978; Driffield and Noor, 1999; Belderbos *et al.*, 2001; Giroud, 2003). Interactions between buyers and suppliers might be limited to a simple "goods for payment" exchange – in which case the likelihood of transfer of other resources is low. As foreign affiliates typically source fewer inputs locally than domestic firms due to preference for intra-firm purchasing or weak local supplier capability or competitiveness, the developmental impact of these linkages is often limited (Turok, 1993: Scotland; Ruane and Görg, 1997: Ireland).

However, where domestic firms are more capable, and when goods and services are location-bound, supplier-specific or customized, then affiliates may form on-going relationships with domestic suppliers or subcontractors (UNCTAD, 2001). If these relationships are intense – i.e. they are more engaging, involving on-going interaction between the firms – they are more likely to involve the diffusion and transfer of resources that contribute to the upgrading of O-advantages in domestic firms. For example, in a study of the relationships between eight foreign affiliates and their 16 subcontractors in Singapore, Poh-Kam

Wong (1992) found that the affiliates had a significant and positive influence on the technological development of their local subcontractors. Affiliates encouraged their domestic subcontractors to upgrade their production capabilities to meet the required standards, and offered technology, information, exposure to good manufacturing processes, and assistance with technological learning to help them do so. The transfer of such resources from the affiliates to domestic suppliers or subcontractors is confirmed by other studies (Halbach, 1989; UNCTAD, 2001; Barrow and Hall, 1995; Dunning, 1998; Papanastassiou and Pearce, 1999; Brown, 1998; Crone and Roper, 2001; Raines *et al.*, 2001; Narula and Marin, 2003; Giroud, 2003).

A few studies have also been extended to include forward linkages (Rodriquez-Clare, 1996; Sun, 1996; Scott-Kennel, 2004), which are formed with domestic customers or agents for distribution, marketing and services (Wright, 1990). Such linkages allow affiliates to draw on the experience of local firms, access established distribution networks and provide on-going support to customers. It is expected that there will also be a certain level of co-operation and information sharing between the firms to facilitate these linkages, which may promote resource and knowledge transfer by the affiliates, such as techniques for optimal product use, corporate marketing ideas, or organizational practices relating to staff training, distribution and after-sales service.

Contractual linkages are formed with domestic firms that undertake licensing or franchising contracts with foreign affiliates. These types of agreements may enable the affiliate to specialize by contracting out non-core activities, to meet host country regulations on local content, or to take advantage of existing local manufacturing capacity or sales outlets. Such agreements typically involve the transfer of codifiable O-advantages and resources, such as product or process technology, marketing practices and brands, equipment, managerial support, training, as well as business practices and procedures. However, contractual agreements are less commonly used in conjunction with FDI (Ietto-Gillies, 1992). Accepted theory asserts that FDI occurs when a TNC exploits O-advantages across national boundaries via internalisation (Dunning, 1993). In other words, FDI is the entry mode chosen when all three elements of the eclectic paradigm, namely; O, L, and I, are present. Contractual linkages, on the other hand, relax the 'I' element of the paradigm by involving external firms. Therefore, where a TNC has already established a wholly-owned subsidiary in the host country for the purposes of internalising O-advantages, it is less likely to use local licensees or franchisees.

Collaborative agreements include any form of non-equity based cooperative agreement among firms, such as strategic alliances, technology development contracts, management contracts, and cooperative marketing agreements (Garcia-Canal *et al.*, 2002). Cost, competitive rivalry or timing considerations lead firms to collaborate, to share unique competences with alliance partners and to engage in mutual development, despite the difficulties associated with this strategy and the risks of losing O-advantages to competitors (Cantwell and Narula, 2001). Affiliates engaged in collaborative linkages may seek specialization in their own areas of expertise, relying on partners for other value-added activities, or the joint development of expertise drawing on the complementary skills of a domestic partner, e.g. in the design of technology or products suited to the local market. Domestic firms may have innovative products that need financial or marketing support from a better-resourced TNC. Both contractual and collaborative linkages are more cooperative in nature, i.e. both firms are likely to contribute to a reciprocal flow of information and resources. However, due to their intensity and focus, collaborative linkages offer the most potential for exchange, sharing and joint development of resources and O-advantages.

If neither indirect nor direct linkage formation occurs in the presence of inward FDI, this is indicative of a foreign enclave. Enclave environments have been experienced in countries operating special economic zones (SEZs), e.g. where foreign presence is high and affiliates are geared towards exporting, relying heavily on inputs from their parent companies or other foreign enterprises operating in the zones (McIntyre *et al.*, 1996; Aitken *et al.*, 1997).

Our review of the literature reveals that a country's progression through the IDP trajectory is determined by the influence of government policy on the development of favourable L-advantages, and then, in later stages, the development of local knowledge-intensive O-advantages. Inward FDI can play an equally important role in the development of these advantages via linkages, where existing levels of domestic capability determine the types and intensity of linkage formation (Giroud and Mirza, 2004). However, few studies consider the potential impact of a range of firm-level linkages as resource transfer mechanisms (but see Scott-Kennel and Enderwick, 2004), nor does the literature explicitly consider how linkages at the firm level might relate to a country's progression through the IDP. We attempt to address these limitations in the second half of this article.

Exploring the black box : linkages and the IDP trajectory

The relationship between the micro-level linkages between foreign affiliates and domestic firms and the macro-level economic development of a host country can be conceptualized in three steps: TNC entry and inter-firm linkage formation, O-advantage augmentation and progression through the stages of the IDP.

Step 1: Entry of a TNC and inter-firm linkage formation

TNC entry into a host economy through inward FDI is typically associated with a bundle of internalized (I_F) foreign ownership-specific advantages (O_F)[2], including products, processes, knowledge, technology and managerial practices as well as the benefits arising from the organization of such advantages internationally. Empirical evidence shows that intra-firm transfer of O_F increases an affiliate's competitiveness and performance in a host country (Dunning, 1993).

---

[2] Where $_F$ = Foreign and $_H$ = Host or Domestic.

But how might inward FDI contribute to the O-advantage augmentation process of domestic firms? Linkages between affiliates and domestic firms create the potential for diffusion or transfer of O_F-advantages, resources and assistance through the indirect or direct transmission mechanisms outlined earlier in this article. The type and intensity of linkage formation are influenced by the O-advantages of an affiliate (O_F) as well at those of domestic firms (O_H); the extent of full or partial internalization (I_F) of O_F-advantages by an affiliate (or by a domestic firm); and the location-specific advantages (L_H) in a host-country.[3] A summary of key relationships is shown in table 1: in the absence of O_H-advantages, an enclave scenario is likely; but as O_H-advantages improve and develop, competitive and transactional linkages occur, and the likelihood of full internalization of O_F-advantages by affiliates (I_F) decreases – eventually leading to a scenario whereby foreign and domestic firms may share resources through collaborative linkages involving only the partial internalization of O-advantages by partners (I_F and I_H).

Table 1. Influence of L_H , I_F and O_H on non-equity inter-firm linkages[a]

	$+L_H$	$+L_H +O_H$	$+L_H+O_H+I_H$
$+I_F$	Enclave	Competitive	
		Transactional	
$-I_F$		Contractual	Collaborative

Source: the authors.

[a] O_F-advantages assumed.

---

[3] These OLI factors are influenced by a number of determinants, including firm strategy, affiliate characteristics such as size, age, motive for investment and autonomy, government policy and economic structure (Giroud and Mirza, 2004).

Table 2 gives a more detailed coverage of the OLI configuration associated with each type of linkage, and the expected impact on O_F-advantage transfer or diffusion. In the discussion that follows, we address each of these linkages in turn.

Under an enclave scenario, O_F-advantages are fully internalized by an affiliate. This may be as a result of weak O_H-advantages, such as insufficiently developed technical capabilities, production capacity or managerial skills (Giroud, 1993). It may also be the result of a TNC's strategy favouring intra-firm linkages over inter-firm linkages. Location-specific variables in the host country (L_H) influence both these factors. For example, host government intervention may inhibit affiliate-domestic firm interaction through the establishment of EPZs as the sole domain of foreign owned firms. In an enclave environment, there is no direct transfer of O_F-advantages by affiliates. The gradual upgrading of O_H is only possible via demonstration effects; the pace of development depends on existing levels of O_H. There is, however, scope for affiliates to upgrade their O_F-advantages in conjunction with opportunities presented by the location-specific advantages of the host country (L_H).

The entry of foreign competitors influences the propensity of domestic firms to upgrade existing O_H-advantages. First and foremost, affiliates seek to protect proprietary assets (O_F) from domestic competitors through full internalization (I_F). Despite the absence of any direct, transactional linkages between firms, however, there is still scope for O_H-advantage upgrading through the effects of competitive pressure on domestic competitors coupled with emulation and demonstration effects. This is more likely where the O-advantages of foreign affiliates (O_F) and those of domestic firms (O_H) are similar in strength, and where location-specific factors (L_H) are supportive of the development of domestic competition. In the absence of such an environment, domestic firms are more likely to become acquisition targets by TNCs, or to be squeezed out of the market by the superior performance of foreign affiliates.

Table 2. Inter-firm linkages and ownership-advantage augmentation

Linkage	OLI configuration	O-advantage transfer (or diffusion)	Expected impact on O-advantage augmentation
Enclave	O_H weak	Diffusion of O_F possible via emulation, demonstration or worker mobility effects	Changes to market/industry structure over time
	L_H unsupportive of local development		Augmentation of O-advantages limited to the affiliate
	Full I_F	No direct transfer of O_F by affiliate	
Competitive	If O_F and O_H dissimilar (O_H weak)	Diffusion of O_F unlikely given weak O_H (capability)	Domestic competitors either do not exist or are insufficiently developed to compete with the affiliate
	L_H unsupportive of local development	No direct transfer of O_F by affiliate	Increase in market concentration, decrease in competition if domestic firms are squeezed out
	Full I_F		Loss/decline of O_H (if present) in favour of O_F due to competitive pressure. O_H may increase in related/supporting industries
	If O_F and O_H similar (O_H strong)	Diffusion of O_F probable via emulation or demonstration effects given strong O_H (capability)	Direct competitive pressure may force upgrading by domestic firm and/or affiliate
	L_H supportive of local development		Former employees may leave to establish their own companies
	Full I_F	No direct transfer of O_F by affiliate	Local competition may prompt hostile action by affiliate (ie. acquisition of O_H)
			Changes to industry structure, market competition over time augments O_H
Transactional	O_H complementary to linkage formation	Forward linkages: O_F transfer likely through assistance, products, marketing specifications, after-sales service etc.	O_F coupled with existing O_H leads to O_H augmentation by domestic firm due to: demands by affiliate for improvement to the quality of service (e.g. agent); assistance and resources (including O_F) given by affiliate to improve domestic agent/customer output; supply of improved variety and quality of
	L_H supportive of local development		

/...

Linkage	OLI configuration	O-advantage transfer (or diffusion)	Expected impact on O-advantage augmentation
	Full or partial I_F possible	Backward linkages: O_F transfer likely in areas of product/process technology, design specifications, quality control, information, etc.	products/services by the affiliate (e.g. supplying a domestic customer with technology that was previously unavailable (also embodies O_F). O_F coupled with existing O_H leads to O_H augmentation by domestic firm due to: demands by affiliate for improvement to the quality of product/service; assistance and resources (including O_F) given by affiliate to improve domestic supplier/ subcontractor output.
Contractual	O_H complementary L_H supportive of local development, possibly not supportive of foreign activity in this area Partial I_F and I_H	Transfer of O_F, unique to the foreign firm but given to local licensees/franchises, such as product/process technology, design specifications, brands, etc.	O_F coupled with existing O_H leads to O_H augmentation by domestic firm due to: the transfer of resources and assistance (including O_F); and the need for the domestic licensee/ franchisee to meet the affiliate's standards and specifications for output.
Collaborative	O_F and O_H strong and complementary L_H supportive of local development Partial I_F and I_H	Reciprocal transfer of O_F and O_H advantages, such as technology, products, processes, expertise, etc.	Collaborative relationship likely to prompt O-advantage augmentation (O_F and O_H) via innovation, technology development, human resource development and sharing of competences by both firms.

Source: the authors.
Note:
O_H = Ownership-specific advantages of host country (domestic) firms.
O_F = Ownership-specific advantages of foreign affiliates.
L_H = Location-specific advantages of host country.
I_F = Internalization-specific advantages of foreign affiliates.
I_H = Internalization-specific advantages of host country (domestic) firms.

If transactional linkages are limited to local sourcing and supply exchanges, the opportunities for resource transfer are low. However, where existing L_H- and O_H-advantages are conducive to more intense inter-firm relationships, there is more potential for transfer of O_F-advantages, resources or assistance to domestic firms via backward and forward linkages. Existing O_H-advantages of domestic firms influence their ability to meet competitive pressure, cater to demand, absorb and adapt new competences, and upgrade existing O_H-advantages (UNCTAD, 1999; Bertschek, 1995; Blomstrom, 1991).

The use of contractual agreements with domestic firms may occur in response to government regulations (e.g. local content regulations), or as part of a specialization strategy by an affiliate. O_H- and L_H-advantages need to be sufficiently well developed. The partial internalization of O_F-advantages occurs via the transfer of production or service related resources. This enables domestic licensees or franchisees to upgrade their existing capabilities and capacity to meet the requirements of TNCs, and to use existing O_H-advantages more competitively. In the case of collaborative agreements, the domestic partner possesses a high level of competency in complementary value-added activities (O_H-advantages) (Chen and Chen, 1998; Madhok and Phene, 2001). An agreement may occur for strategic reasons, for mutual exploitation and/or development of O_F- and O_H-advantages. Collaborative linkages involve a reciprocal inter-firm transfer of O_F-advantages and O_H-advantages (Perez, 1997). Partners may also engage in the joint development of new O-advantages in the host economy.

Step 2: Ownership-advantage augmentation

Figure 1 shows the process of O-advantage augmentation as a result of inter-firm linkage formation. The entry of a TNC into a host economy at time t is associated with the introduction of O_F-advantages to the host economy. Under enclave conditions, only the affiliate stands to benefit from the upgrading of its O_F-advantages in time period $t+1$. It does so by employing the traditional TNC strategy of full internalization $(+I_F)$ – in other words, by exploiting its firm-specific assets in combination with host economy L-advantages (L_H). The same strategy is employed under competitive conditions; however, the existence or emergence of domestic firm O_H-advantages offers the capacity for O_H upgrading via competition and demonstration effects (represented as t+x due to the expected time lag effect of indirect linkages).

If O_H–advantages are sufficiently strong to encourage direct transactional linkage formation, there is the potential for the transfer of certain O_F-advantages by affiliates and subsequently upgrading of O_H. The strength of O_H t+1 depends on the extent of I_F by affiliates. I_F, in turn, is determined by the intensity of the linkage formation – whether affiliates engage with domestic suppliers and customers in on-going relationships.

Contractual and collaborative linkages rely on strong O_H- and L_H-advantages as well as partial I_F by affiliates. The augmentation of O-advantages by both foreign affiliates and domestic firms (O_F t+1 + O_H t+1) is made possible by the reciprocal exchange of resources, as well as joint organizational learning and cooperation. Collaborative linkages also present a high likelihood of mutual development and the creation of ownership-specific advantages by both firms working together (as shown by (O_F + O_H) t+1 in figure 1).

In summary, the extent of O-advantage augmentation is dependent on the existing capabilities of domestic firms and the extent to which the diffusion and/or transfer of O_F-

Figure 1. Ownership-advantage augmentation process

Inter-firm linkages		OLI configuration (t)	O-advantage augmentation (t+1)	Linkage intensity
Direct	Collaborative	$= O_{Ft} - I_{Ft} + L_{Ht} + O_{Ht} - I_H$ ⟶	$= O_{F\,t+1} + O_{H\,t+1} + (O_F + O_H)_{t+1}$	High
	Contractual	$= O_{Ft} - I_{Ft} + L_{Ht} + O_{Ht}$ ⟶	$= O_{F\,t+1} + O_{H\,t+1}$	
	Transactional	$= O_{Ft} +/- I_{Ft} + L_{Ht} + O_{Ht}$ ⟶	$= O_{F\,t+1} +/- O_{H\,t+1}$	
Indirect	Competitive Demonstration	$= O_{Ft} + I_{Ft} + L_{Ht} +/- O_{Ht}$ ⟶	$= O_{F\,t+1} +/- O_{H\,t+x}$	
	Enclave	$= O_{Ft} + I_{Ft} + L_{Ht}$ ⟶	$= O_{F\,t+1}$	Low

Source: the authors.
Note: t = time

advantages occurs. From our analysis, we can classify inter-firm linkages according to their degree of intensity: from low to high. Indirect linkages are low intensity due to the lack of direct resource transfer among firms; transactional linkages are moderate (i.e. local sourcing) to high intensity (i.e. subcontracting), depending on the extent of resource transfer; and contractual and collaborative linkages are high intensity due to the potential for reciprocal resource exchange.

Step 3: IDP stages

Due to the high number of possible OLI permutations, individual country trajectories and possible linkage combinations taken by affiliates, it is difficult to map an exact relationship between micro-level inter-firm linkages, changes to OLI and stages of the IDP. However, we have attempted to show the interplay between these variables in figure 2, which illustrates how linkages of different intensity are associated with different stages of the IDP, as well as the expected changes to the OLI configuration over time.

Figure 2. OLI configuration, linkage intensity and IDP stages

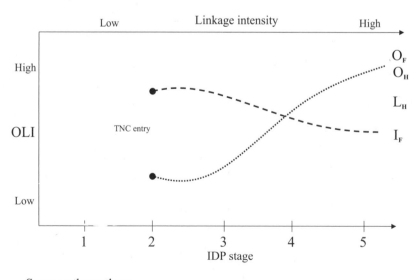

Source: the authors.

Countries in Stage 1 of the IDP are unlikely to achieve any linkages due to the poor accessibility of L_H-advantages, weak O_H, and negligible FDI. At best, the entry of TNCs into enclave environments may encourage weak demonstration or worker mobility effects. The government acts as the major driver for progression into Stage 2 by developing L_H-advantages, such as basic infrastructure, education and market-oriented institutions. Resource seeking inward FDI emerges to take advantage of natural assets and low labour costs. If protectionist policies are in force, they encourage the entry of import-substituting, market seeking investment. Inward FDI directed to countries in Stage 2 is associated with the intra-firm (parent firm to affiliate) transfer of intangible assets, such as technology, trademarks and managerial/organizational skills (Dunning and Narula, 1996). Initially, internalization (I_F) of such O_F-advantages is high, as affiliates have little to gain from working closely with domestic firms, although low intensity linkages such as local sourcing and the supply of standardized goods and services may occur. Competition between affiliates and domestic firms also encourages internalization (I_F) by affiliates.

However, as countries shift from Stage 2 to Stage 3, a process driven by both government policies and FDI activities, we can see the gradual evolution of the OLI configuration in figure 2. L-advantages continue to improve, encouraging both market seeking and efficiency seeking inward FDI. However, the most crucial change is the upgrading of O_H, in particular created assets such as human skills and knowledge, innovation and technology. This has a number of beneficial effects. First, it encourages linkage formation between affiliates and domestic firms. Second, it improves the absorptive capacity of domestic firms, enabling them to benefit more from both demonstration effects and transactional linkages. Third, it enables domestic firms to compete more successfully with locally based affiliates in existing or emerging industries.

As O_H-advantages continue to develop, competition in selected industries intensifies, and affiliates introduce more sophisticated O_F-advantages to compete against local competitors (Dunning and Narula, 1996). This may be achieved through intra-firm transfer of technology and innovation from parent firm, increased emphasis on the international coordination of advantages, and/or increased local development, innovation and adaptation of products and processes by affiliates in a host country. Domestic firms, if not targets of strategic asset-seeking investments by affiliates, are often able to participate in the periphery of this local development activity. Many also engage in outward FDI to countries in Stages 1 and 2, which helps counter rising labour costs at home, or even to later stage countries to acquire assets and capabilities (Barry, Görg and McDowell, 2002; Chen and Chen, 1998; Makino *et al.*, 2002). As figure 2 shows, the combination of these effects prompts the upgrading of both O_H and O_F advantages, as full I_F is relaxed. Affiliates become more embedded in the local economy via higher intensity linkages with domestic firms that involve the transfer of resources and assistance.

These trends continue with the shift to Stage 4. Stage 4 countries are distinguished by developed-country status, high levels of O_H- and L_H-advantages and outward FDI based on created assets and capital-intensive activities (Dunning, Kim and Lin, 2001). Governments adopt the role of facilitator of economic activity, while inward, and especially outward FDI, are important to the continued upgrading of O_H-advantages. Inward FDI is increasingly strategic asset seeking or asset augmenting in nature. In addition to mergers and acquisitions, affiliates engage in strategic alliances and other collaborative arrangements with domestic firms in order to access O_H- and L_H-advantages embodied in host country firms and industries. TNCs are increasingly looking for locations that contribute to asset augmentation through complementary technology, innovation, capabilities, and competences (Narula and Dunning, 2000). Rather than the simple transfer of ownership advantages that occurs via acquisition, collaboration presents the opportunity for both firms to upgrade O-advantages. Figure 2 shows how the internalization (I_F) of O-advantages declines with the transition to Stage 5 (we have not shown I_H, but this would show a similar trend), as affiliates engage in more high intensity linkages with domestic firms.

Outward FDI traditionally surpasses inward FDI at Stage 4, and is motivated by trade, market, and asset seeking objectives. Growing international experience and the cross-border organization and acquisition of resources contributes to O_H-advantage upgrading. Alternative trajectories, where outward FDI still trails inward FDI, are associated with the underdevelopment of O_H (Duran and Ubeda, 2001). However, the transition to Stage 5 requires the upgrading of O_H in line with other Stage 5 countries. Figure 2 indicates that, as countries move towards Stage 5, the differences among O_F- and O_H-advantages converge and start to level off. This is evidence of cross hauling of investment among countries in Stage 5, as O_H- and O_F-advantages become more complementary and competition is increasingly centred on product differentiation and created intangible knowledge assets. Inward FDI from earlier stage countries seeking to acquire or locate in close proximity to O_H-advantages may also contribute to linkages and resource exchange. Over time, there also may be evidence of the hollowing out of O_H-advantages due to reverse spillovers (Driffield and Love, 2003). Thus, while still having high levels of competition and transaction linkages, Stage 5 countries are likely to achieve higher intensity linkages than achieved in Stage 4, particularly via inter-firm collaboration.

Exploring the black box of the IDP : discussion and concluding remarks

This article investigates the black box of the IDP – how domestic firms upgrade their resources and capabilities via linkages with foreign affiliates, thus eventually being able to undertake outward FDI independently. Our primary objective is to explain the workings of this black box: first by investigating the types and intensity of resource transmission mechanisms, then by exploring relationships between linkage type, changes to the OLI configuration and progression on the IDP trajectory by a host economy.

The first contribution of this article is its theoretical investigation of non-equity, inter-firm resource transfer mechanisms between foreign affiliates and domestic firms. The impact of FDI on host country firms can be better understood by evaluating the extent and intensity of a wide range of non-equity linkages – demonstration, competitive, transactional, contractual and collaborative. The inclusion of the complete spectrum of possible transmission mechanisms as well as their intensity captures the likely extent of diffusion and transfer of O_F-advantages, enabling the extrapolation of the outcomes for domestic firm development.

The second contribution of this article is its explanation of how the process of upgrading of O_F- and O_H-specific advantage might occur over time at the micro level. This process differs according to the OLI configuration of foreign entrants, which the authors expanded to include the ownership-specific advantages of host country firms (O_H) and alternative organizational routes such as inter-firm linkages and collaboration. We suggest that linkage type and intensity influence the OLI configuration and as well as the process of upgrading.

Third, our investigation suggests that in addition to GDP per capita and other macro-level measures of development, firm-level indicators (such as the intensity of linkage formation and domestic firm capability) are useful to evaluate a country's progression on the IDP. Specifically, our article provides support for the notion suggested by Duran and Ubeda (2001) that outward FDI at the firm level might be more closely linked to local competence (O_H) development, rather than a level of GDP or specific IDP stage. It also addresses other methodological problems raised with regard to the use of the aggregate measure of inward and outward FDI stock (NOI). Outward FDI from a host country may not be undertaken by indigenous firms, but by foreign affiliates, thus perhaps overestimating the level of host country firm capability at later stages of the IDP (Bellak, 2001). Thus, we emphasize the importance of understanding the extent of affiliate-domestic firm interaction and whether this leads to the upgrading of host country firm capabilities (and, ultimately, outward FDI), rather than just affiliate upgrading.

This distinction is masked in most aggregate industry-level studies of linkages and spillovers.

Fourth, we support literature that stresses the importance of mutually reinforcing host country characteristics – government policy, infrastructure and education, the attraction of appropriate inward FDI, and the development of O_H-advantages (Ozawa and Castello, 2001; Narula, 1996). Economic upgrading at the macro level is the result of a complex set of relationships between the O_F-advantages accompanying inward investment, L_H-specific advantages and domestic firm O_H-advantages, and the means by which firms organize these advantages at the micro level. We find that inter-firm linkage formation is another important contributor to a virtuous cycle of development; but in order to obtain maximum benefit from inward FDI, the simultaneous development of L_H- and O_H-advantages is crucial. It follows, therefore, that not only do host countries exhibit different propensities for linkage formation in different stages of the IDP, but also that linkage formation is less likely and less beneficial for earlier stage countries, where governments play a more important role in the initial development of L_H- and O_H- advantages (Dunning and Narula, 1996). Types of FDI and types of linkages (and their intensity) evolve as the OLI configuration changes. This, in turn, prompts the critical transition process from earlier stages to later stages of the IDP trajectory for a host country. For countries shifting from Stage 2 to 3, linkages are among a set of factors driving development. In the shift to Stages 4 and 5, where the need for knowledge-based assets is paramount, linkages take on more prominence as alternative asset augmentation mechanisms. This finding is supported by previous research that found that countries with higher levels of structural, technological and human capital development benefit more from inward FDI spillovers (Borensztein *et al.*, 1998; Bengoa and Sanchez-Robles, 2003).

In conclusion, the investigation of micro-level mechanisms of host country development in the form of non-equity inter-firm linkages improves our understanding of how host country firms upgrade their O_H-advantages, enabling them to contribute to host country economic development at the macro level. Specifically, we propose that the contribution of inward FDI to a country's stage of economic development is positively related to the degree of linkage intensity at the firm level. Linkage intensity can be defined as the extent to which firms engage or interact with each other through transactional, contractual or collaborative linkages. Central to the concept of intensity, therefore, is the extent to which firms exchange, transfer, share or develop resources via linkages. Our theoretical investigation of inter-firm linkages supports the notion that foreign affiliates exert developmental impacts at the micro (firm) level that are obscured by macro-level analysis.

Areas for future research include testing of the relationships between linkage intensity, the extent of externalization of O-advantages by affiliates and the development of O_H-advantages by domestic firms, and the relationship between O_H-advantage augmentation and a host country's progression through the stages of the IDP trajectory. ■

References

Aitken, Brian, Gordon H. Hanson and Ann E. Harrison (1997). "Spillovers, foreign investment, and export behavior", *Journal of International Economics*, 43, pp. 103-132.

_____ and Ann E. Harrison (1999). "Do domestic firms benefit from direct foreign investment? Evidence from Venezuela", *American Economic Review,* 89(3), pp. 605-618.

Akoorie, Michèle M. E. (1996). "New Zealand: the economic development of a resource-rich economy", in John H. Dunning and Rajneesh Narula, eds., *Foreign Direct Investment and Governments: Catalysts for Economic Restructuring.* (London and New York: Routledge), pp. 174-206.

Barrell, Ray and Nigel Pain (1997). "Foreign direct investment, technological change, and economic growth within Europe", *Economic Journal,* 107 (445), pp. 1770-1786.

Barry, Frank, Holger Görg and Andrew McDowell (2003). "Outward FDI and the investment development path in a late-industrialising economy: evidence from Ireland", *Regional Studies,* 37(4), pp. 341-349.

Barrow, Michael and Mike Hall (1995). "The impact of a large multinational organization on a small local economy", *Regional Studies,* 29(7), pp. 635-653.

Belderbos, René, Giovanni Capannelli and Kyoji Fukao (2001). "Backward vertical linkages of foreign manufacturing affiliates: evidence from Japanese multinationals", *World Development,* 29(1), pp. 189-208.

Bellak, Christian (2001). "The Austrian investment development path", *Transnational Corporations,* 10(2), pp. 107-134.

Bengoa, Marta and Blanca Sanchez-Robles (2003). "Foreign direct investment, economic freedom and growth: new evidence from Latin America", *European Journal of Political Economy,* 19(3), pp. 529-545.

Bertschek, Irene (1995). "Product and process innovation as a response to increasing imports and foreign direct investment", *The Journal of Industrial Economics,* XLIII (December), pp. 341-357.

Blomström, Magnus (1991). "Host country benefits of foreign investment", in Donald G. McFetridge, ed., *Foreign Investment, Technology and Economic Growth* (Toronto and London: Toronto University Press), pp. 93-109.

_____ and Ari Kokko (1998). "Multinational corporations and spillovers", *Journal of Economic Surveys,* 12(3), pp. 247-278.

Borensztein, Eduardo, Jose De Gregorio and Jong-Wha Lee (1998). "How does foreign direct investment affect economic growth?", *Journal of International Economics,* 45(1), pp. 1115-135.

Brown, Ross (1998). "Electronics foreign direct investment in Singapore: a study of local linkages in "Winchester City", *European Business Review,* 98(4), pp. 196-210.

Buckley, Peter J. and Mark Casson (1976). *The Future of the Multinational Enterprise* (London: Macmillan).

_____ and Mark C. Casson (1985). *The Economic Theory of the Multinational Enterprise* (London: Macmillan).

_____ and Mark C. Casson (1998) "Analyzing foreign market entry strategies: extending the internalization approach", *Journal of International Business Studies,* 29(3), pp. 539-561.

_____ and Francisco B. Castro (1998). "The investment development path: the case of Portugal", *Transnational Corporations,* 7(1), pp. 1-15.

Buckley, Rita (2004). "Multinational enterprises (MNEs) and productivity improvements to domestic firms through worker mobility: an empirical model of the Irish Software Industry ". Paper presented to the Department of Economics, Waikato Management School, University of Waikato, mimeo.

Cantwell, John and Simona Immarino (2000). "Multinational corporations and the location of technological innovation in the UK regions", *Regional Studies,* 34(3), pp. 317-332.

_____ and Rajneesh Narula (2001). "The eclectic paradigm in the global economy", *International Journal of the Economics of Business,* 8(2), pp. 155-172.

_____ and Lucia Piscitello (2002). "The location of technological activities of MNCs in European regions: the role of spillovers and local competencies", *Journal of International Management,* 8, pp. 69-96.

Castro, Francisco B. (2004). "Foreign direct investment in a late industrialising country: the Portugese IDP revisited" (Porto: Universidade do Porto), mimeo.

Chen, Homin, and Tain-Jy Chen (1998). "Foreign direct investment as a strategic linkage", *Thunderbird International Business Review,* 40(1), pp. 13-31.

Coe, David T., Elhanan Helpman and Alexander Hoffmeister (1997). "North-South R&D spillovers", *The Economic Journal,* 107(January), pp. 134-149.

Crone, Mike and Stephen Roper (2001). "Local learning from multinational plants: knowledge transfers in the supply chain", *Regional Studies,* 35(6), pp. 535-48.

De Mello, Luiz R. Jr. (1997). "Foreign direct investment in developing countries and growth: a selective survey", *The Journal of Development Studies,* 34(1), pp. 1-34.

Driffield, Nigel and James Love (2003). "Foreign direct investment, technology sourcing and reverse spillovers", *The Manchester School. Manchester,* 71(6), pp. 659-673.

_____ and Abd Halim Mohd Noor (1999). "Foreign direct investment and local input linkages in Malaysia", *Transnational Corporations,* 8(3), pp. 1-24.

Dunning, John H. (1980). "Toward an eclectic theory of international production: some empirical tests", *Journal of International Business Studies,* 11(1), pp. 9-31.

_____ (1981). "Explaining the international direct investment position of countries: towards a dynamic or development approach", *Weltwirtschaftliches Archiv,* 117, pp. 30-64.

_____ (1986). "The investment development cycle revisited", *Weltwirtshaftliches Archiv,* 122, pp. 667-677.

_____ (1988). "The eclectic paradigm of international production: a restatement and some possible extensions", *Journal of International Business Studies,* 19, pp. 1-32.

_____ (1993). *Multinational Enterprises and the Global Economy* (Workingham, England: Addison-Wesley Publishing Company).

_____ (1995). "Reappraising the eclectic paradigm in an age of alliance capitalism", *Journal of International Business Studies,* 26(3), pp. 461-491.

_____ (1998). *American Investment in British Manufacturing Industry* (London and New York: Routledge).

_____, ed. (2000). *Regions, Globalization, and the Knowledge-based Economy* (Oxford and New York: Oxford University Press).

_____ (2001). "The eclectic (OLI) paradigm of international production: past, present and future", *Journal of the Economics of Business,* 8(2), pp. 173-190.

_____, C. S. Kim and D. J. Lin (2001). "Incorporating trade into the investment development path", *Oxford Development Studies,* 29, pp. 145-154.

_____ and Sarianna Lundan (1998). "The geographical sources of competitiveness of multinational enterprises: an econometric analysis", *International Business Review,* 7(2), pp. 115-133.

_____ and Rajneesh Narula (1996). *Foreign Direct Investment and Governments: Catalysts for Economic Restructuring* (London and New York: Routledge).

Durán, Juan J. and Fernando Ubeda (2001). "The investment development path: a new empirical approach and some theoretical issues", *Transnational Corporations,* 10(2), pp. 1-34.

_____ (2003). "A dynamic analysis of the inward and outward direct investment of the newly developed countries". Paper presented to the 29th Annual Conference of the European International Business Academy, Copenhagen, mimeo.

Engelbrecht, Hans-Jürgen (1997). "International R&D spillovers, human capital and productivity in OECD economies: an empirical investigation", *European Economic Review,* 41, pp. 1479-1488.

Enright, Michael J. (2000). "Regional clusters and multinational enterprises: independence, dependence or interdependence?", *International Studies of Management and Organization,* 30(2), pp. 114-38.

Garcia-Canal, Esteban, Cristina Lopez Duarte, Josep Rialp Criado and Ana Valdes Llaneza (2002). "Accelerating international expansion through global alliances: a typology of cooperative strategies", *Journal of World Business,* 37(2), pp. 91-107.

Ghoshal, Sumantra and Christopher A. Bartlett (1990). "The multinational corporation as an interorganizational network", *Academy of Management Review,* 15(4), pp. 603-625.

Giroud, Axèle (2003). *Transnational Corporations, Technology and Economic Development: Backward Linkages and Knowledge Transfer in South-East Asia* (Cheltenham, UK: Edward Elgar).

_____ and H. Mirza (2004). "Multinational enterprises and local input linkages in Southeast Asia". Paper presented to the Academy of International Business Conference 11-13 July, Stockholm, mimeo.

Görg, Holger and Eric Strobl (2002). "Multinational companies and indigenous development: an empirical analysis", *European Economic Review*, 46, pp. 1305-1322.

_____ (2003). "Multinational companies, technology spillovers and plant survival", *Scandinavian Journal of Economics*, 105(4), pp. 581-595.

Griffith, David A. and Michael G. Harvey (2001). "A resource perspective of global dynamic capabilities", *Journal of International Business Studies*, 32(3), pp. 597-606.

Guisinger, Stephen (2001). "From OLI to OLMA: incorporating higher levels of environmental and structural complexity into the eclectic paradigm", *International Journal of the Economics of Business*, 8(2), pp. 257-272.

Håkansson, Lars and Jan Johanson (1993). "The network as a governance structure", In G. Grabher, ed., *The Embedded Firm* (London and Boston: Routledge), pp. 35-51.

Halbach, A. J. (1989). "Multinational enterprises and subcontracting in the Third World: a study of inter-industrial linkages" (Geneva, ILO), mimeo.

Holm, Ulf and Torben Pedersen, eds. (2000). *The Emergence and Impact of MNC Centres of Excellence: A Subsidiary Perspective* (London and New York: MacMillan Press).

Ietto-Gillies, Grazia (1992). *International Production Trends, Theories, Effects* (Cambridge: Polity Press).

Ivarsson, Inge (1999). "Competitive industry clusters and inward TNC investment: the case of Sweden", *Regional Studies*, 33(1), pp. 37-49.

Khawar, Mariam (2003). "Productivity and foreign direct investment: evidence from Mexico", *Journal of Economic Studies*, 30(1), pp. 66-76.

Kogut, Bruce and Udo Zander (1993). "Knowledge of the firm and the evolutionary theory of the multinational corporation", *Journal of International Business Studies*, 24(4), pp. 625-645.

Kokko, Ari (1994). "Technology, market characteristics, and spillovers", *Journal of Development Economics*, 43(2), pp. 279-93.

_____, Ruben Tansini and Mario C. Zejan (1996). "Local technology capability and productivity spillovers from FDI in the Uruguayan manufacturing sector", *Journal of Development Studies*, 32(4), pp. 602-612.

Kuemmerle, Walter (1996). "The drivers of foreign direct investment into research and development: an empirical investigation", *Journal of International Business Studies,* 30(1), pp. 1-24.

Lundan, Sarianna, ed. (2002). *Network Knowledge in International Business.* (Cheltenham: Edward Elgar).

_____ and John Hagedoorn (2001). "Alliances, acquisitions and multinational advantage", *International Journal of the Economics of Business*, 8(2), pp. 229-242.

Madhok, Anoop and Anupama Phene (2001). "The co-evolutional advantage: strategic management theory and the eclectic paradigm", *International Journal of the Economics of Business*, 8(2), pp. 243-256.

Makino, Shige, Chung-Ming Lau and Rhy-Song Yeh (2002). "Asset-exploitation versus asset-seeking: implications for location choice of foreign direct investment from newly industrialized economies", *Journal of International Business Studies,* 33(3), pp. 403-421.

Markusen, James R. and Anthony J. Venables (1999). "Foreign direct investment as a catalyst for industrial development", *European Economic Review,* 43, pp. 335-356.

McAleese, D. and D. McDonald (1978). "Employment growth and the development of linkages in foreign-owned and domestic manufacturing enterprises", *Oxford Bulletin of Economics and Statistics,* 40(4), pp. 321-340.

Narula, Rajneesh (1996). *Multinational Investment and Economic Structure: Globalisation and Competitiveness* (London and New York: Routledge).

_____ and John. H. Dunning (2000). "Industrial development, globalization and multinational enterprises: new realities for developing countries", *Oxford Development Studies*, 28(2), pp. 141-167.

_____ and Anabel Marin (2003). "FDI spillovers, absorptive capacities and human capital development: evidence from Argentina", *MERIT Research Memorandum 2003-016*, mimeo.

_____ and Bert Sadowski (2002). "Technology catch-up and strategic technology partnering in developing countries", *International Journal of Technology Management*, 23(6), pp. 599-617.

McIntyre, John, Rajneesh Narula and Len Trevino (1996). "The role of export processing zones for host countries and multinationals: a mutually beneficial relationship?", *The International Trade Journal,* X(4), pp. 435-465.

Ostry, Sylvia and Michael Gestrin (1993). "Foreign direct investment, technology transfer and the innovation-network model", *Transnational Corporations,* 2(3), pp. 7-30.

Ozawa, Terutomo (1996). "Japan: the macro-IDP, meso-IDPs and the technology development path (TDP)", in John H. Dunning and Raneesh Narula, eds., *Foreign Direct Investment and Governments: Catalysts for Economic Restructuring* (London and New York: Routledge), pp. 142-173.

_____ and Sergio Castello (2001). "Toward an 'international business' paradigm of endogenous growth: multinationals and governments as co-endogenisers", *International Journal of the Economics of Business,* 8(2), pp. 211-228.

Papanastassiou, Marina and Robert Pearce (1999). *Multinationals, Technology and National Competitiveness* (Cheltenham: Edward Elgar).

Pedersen, Kurt (2003). "The eclectic paradigm: a new deal?", *Journal of International Business and Economy*, pp. 15-27.

Perez, Tommaso (1997). "Multinational enterprises and technological spillovers: an evolutionary model", *Journal of Evolutionary Economics,* 7, pp. 169-192.

Raines, Phil, Ivan Turok and Ross Brown (2001). "Growing global: foreign direct investment and the internationalization of local suppliers in Scotland", *European Planning Studies,* 9(8), pp. 965-979.

Rodriguez-Clare, André (1996). "Multinationals, linkages, and economic development", *American Economic Review,* 86(4), pp. 852-873.

Ruane, Frances and Holger Görg (1997). "The impact of foreign direct investment on sectoral adjustment in the Irish economy", *National Institute Economic Review,* 160(April), pp. 76-86.

Rugman, Alan (1980). "Internalization as a general theory of foreign direct investment: a reappraisal of the literature", *Weltwirtschaftliches Archiv,* 116, pp. 365-379.

_____ and Alain Verbeke (2001). "Subsidiary-specific advantages in multinational enterprises", *Strategic Management Journal,* 22, pp. 237-250.

Sadik, Ali T. and Ali A. Bolbol (2001). "Capital flows, FDI, and technology spillovers: evidence from Arab countries", *World Development,* 29(12), pp. 2111-2126.

Scott-Kennel, Joanna (2004). "Foreign direct investment: a catalyst for local firm development?", *European Journal of Development Research,* 16(3), pp. 624-652.

_____ and P. Enderwick (2004). "Inter-firm alliance and network relationships and the eclectic paradigm of international production: an exploratory analysis of quasi-internalisation at the subsidiary level", *International Business Review,* 3(4), pp. 425-445.

Sun, Haishun (1996). "Direct foreign investment and linkage effects: the experience of China", *Asian Economies,* 25(1), pp. 5-28.

Teece, David (1992). "Competition, cooperation and innovation: organisational arrangements for regimes of rapid technological progress", *Journal of Economic Behaviour and Organization,* 18, pp. 1-25.

Turok, Ivan. (1993). "Inward investment and local linkages: how deeply embedded is 'Silicon Glen'?", *Regional Studies,* 27(5), pp. 401-417.

United Nations Conference on Trade and Development (UNCTAD) (1995). *World Investment Report 1995: Transnational Corporations and Competitiveness* (New York and Geneva: United Nations), United Nations publication, Sales No. E.95.II.A.4.

_____ (1999). *World Investment Report 1999: Foreign Direct Investment and the Challenge of Development* (New York and Geneva: United Nations), United Nations publication, Sales No. E.99.II.D.3.

_____ (2001). *World Investment Report 2001: Promoting Linkages* (New York and Geneva: United Nations), United Nations publication, Sales No. E.01.II.D.12.

Wong, Poh-Kam (1992). "Technological development through subcontracting linkages: evidence from Singapore", *Scandinavian International Business Review,* 1(3), pp. 28-40.

Wright, David (1990). "A study of the employment effects and other benefits of collaboration between multinational enterprises and small-scale enterprises" (Geneva: International Labour Office), mimeo.

Zhang, Kevin Honglin (2001). "Does foreign direct investment promote economic growth? Evidence from East Asia and Latin America", *Contemporary Economic Policy,* 19(2), pp. 175-186.

BOOK REVIEWS

Money Markets and Politics: A Study of European Financial Integration and Monetary Policy Options

Jens Forssbæck and Lars Oxelheim
(Cheltenham, Glos., Edward Elgar, 2003), 290 pages

With the growing internationalization of banks and businesses and the evolution of information technology, the last decades have witnessed an increasing integration of national financial markets worldwide. This, in turn, is thought to constrain domestic authorities in their implementation of economic policy and, in particular, of monetary policy because a more open and sophisticated financial sector could weaken "monetary policy transmission by the continuous supply of substitutes to central bank money" (p. 240). So whether or not increased "globalization" of financial markets affects monetary policy choices across countries is an important issue.

The present book seeks to address precisely this question in a European context. It studies the linkages between capital mobility (a proxy for financial integration) and monetary policy implementation according to different institutional arrangements: membership to the European Union (EU) or European Monetary Union (EMU) or different exchange rate regimes. The analytical framework chosen by the authors for exploring such linkages is the "inconsistent trinity" hypothesis. Basically, the theory states that only two of the three key objectives of policymakers (i.e. capital mobility, monetary autonomy and a fixed exchange rate) can be achieved simultaneously over a given period of time. This theory is, therefore, a natural starting point for researchers who wish to investigate if financial integration constrains countries in their monetary policy choices, and if this varies across different exchange rate regimes.

Focusing on 11 small, open European economies over the past two decades (seven members of EMU, two members of the EU but outside EMU, and two outside the EU), this book comprises a set of eight chapters organized in two main parts: one that focuses on the development of *domestic* markets and monetary policies, and a second that deals with the *international* interactions between financial markets and monetary policies.

The opening chapter presents the layout of the book, and makes a good job of motivating the questions addressed by the book. Overall, I think that the book succeeds in delivering what it promises. In what follows, I review each of the different chapters, and conclude with an overall evaluation and what I consider to be the main contributions and omissions.

The first part of the book contains three chapters describing the *domestic* markets of each country over the past two decades, where the countries are classified into subgroups according to their EU/EMU membership. This classification allows an assessment of whether countries that belong to the same subgroup share similar characteristics, or, in other words, if *institutional* integration correlates with *economic* and *financial* integration as one would expect. Contrary to expectations, the analysis reveals considerable variations between, but also *within*, subgroups of countries, leading the authors to conclude that the "institutional integration within the EU has *political* rather than *economic* roots" (p. 41). Countries are shown to differ substantially in terms of economic and financial development, openness to international trade and investment or labour mobility (chapter two), domestic money market structures (chapter three) or in the way monetary policy is implemented (chapter four).

As an international economist, I am particularly interested in the second part of the book which deals with *international* issues, and investigates the different components of the "inconsistent trinity" hypothesis. I really enjoyed reading all the chapters, not least because of their international dimension, but also because they are much less descriptive than those in the first part of the book and present a few empirical models that yield interesting results.

Chapter five provides a detailed overview and graphical description of the different exchange rate regimes across countries, and classifies the different regimes into a few broad categories (flexible, semi-fixed, fixed). This classification enables the analysis, in the following chapters, of the degree of international financial integration (proxied by capital mobility) and of monetary autonomy (two objectives of the "inconsistent trinity") under different nominal exchange rate regimes (the third objective).

Chapters six and seven are, in my opinion, the most interesting contributions. The purpose of chapter six is to estimate the degree of capital mobility by regressing cross-country interest rate differentials on (expected) exchange rate changes (where Germany, the United States and the G5 are used as benchmark countries). The results from four different models, which basically test different versions of the uncovered interest rate parity hypothesis (depending on assumptions about risk neutrality, persistence in interest rate differentials, or on the existence of a common long-run trend), are of significant interest. The findings are very heterogeneous across country-pairs but, on average, indicate an increasing integration of financial markets over time. However, this behaviour of interest rate differentials does not vary systematically across country subgroups or exchange rate regimes, providing "another indication that institutional integration is predicated on political rather than economic considerations" (p. 183).

Chapter seven focuses on the third and final component of the "inconsistent trinity", i.e. monetary policy autonomy. In that chapter, the authors try to determine if the eleven economies are "policy-takers", i.e. whether their monetary policies (proxied by interest rates and monetary aggregates) are determined and/ or influenced by those of larger foreign countries, and whether the results vary across institutional regimes. Three empirical models are thus estimated: the first estimates the elasticities of small countries' domestic interest rates to those of foreign benchmark countries; the second is a bivariate Granger causality test which identifies the degree of asymmetry in the transmission of monetary policy; and the third is a multivariate model that enables the consideration of all possible relationships between all variables. The results from the three approaches are relatively consistent with each other, and indicate some asymmetry in the transmission of monetary policy (the countries are, therefore, policy-takers and thus have lost some autonomy in domestic monetary policy), but with no systematic variation across country subgroups or exchange rate regimes. In all, the main conclusion that emerges from all these tests is that "the degree of monetary policy autonomy is a reflection of financial integration […] in that it is gradually washed away as domestic financial markets become increasingly integrated" (pp. 248-249). Finally, chapter eight summarizes in detail the main contributions and findings of the book.

Overall, this topical book is a valuable contribution, providing interesting and detailed analyses of the developments in financial, monetary and foreign exchange markets across countries, as well as more sophisticated sections that use empirical tools for exploration and modelling. The originality of the approach chosen for the analysis, the diversity of the topics covered and the breadth of the information collected are clearly the book's primary strength. The conclusion that monetary integration in Europe is primarily explained by political factors as opposed to economic factors, as traditionally claimed, is an original and provocative contribution to the literature.

Regarding the possible omissions and limitations, one aspect that is unfortunately not dealt with in the book is the analysis of monetary and financial integration of the new EU member countries. Given that the focus is on small and open European economies, it would have been interesting to include in the sample at least some of those new member countries. Investigating their degree of financial integration and/or money market structure over the past decades (or over a shorter time period in the case of data unavailability) would have enabled the assessment of how these countries compare to original EU or EMU countries, and to draw policy implications regarding EU enlargement. In my opinion, this is the main omission from the book.

Besides, in order to examine whether capital mobility and monetary autonomy differ across country subgroups or exchange rate regimes, the authors simply compare the estimated coefficients obtained from univariate regressions for each country-pair. The results would gain in precision and credibility if the models were instead estimated over all country-pairs pooled together, and included interaction terms to capture different country subgroups or exchange rate regimes.

Finally, given the huge differences that exist within country subgroups, it would be appropriate to further distinguish, within the EMU subgroup, those countries that belong to the "core" EU (Belgium and the Netherlands) from those that joined the EU at a later date (with, for instance, Ireland, Greece and Portugal on the one hand, and Austria and Finland on the other). It seems obvious to me that these countries are different in many respects, since most recent members of the EU are generally less integrated as compared to the founding members of the EC.

To sum up, I think the main audience for this book are academic researchers and students of international macroeconomics or of political science, policymakers and financial market participants, or anyone interested in the subject of monetary and financial integration from a policy perspective.

Natalie Chen
Department of Economics
University of Warwick and CEPR
United Kingdom

International Political Risk Management:
The Brave New World

Theodore H. Moran, editor
(Washington D.C., The World Bank Group, 2004),
xi+238 pages

During the 1990s, as the growth of foreign direct investment continued to exceed the growth of the world economy, emerging market countries aggressively sought to attract transnational corporations (TNCs). This development spurred growth in the political risk insurance (PRI) industry[1]. Formerly dominated by government agencies, the industry grew in size, sophistication and number of players, as private insurance providers increased their presence. During this boom decade, several private risk insurance companies, such as Zurich Emerging Markets Solutions and Sovereign Risk Insurance, entered the market, while established companies, such as Lloyds and AIG, substantially expanded their political risk insurance activities.

The market thus blossomed significantly towards the end of millennium, before being hit by a sequence of shocks, beginning with the Asian currency crisis of 1997, followed by the information technology bubble burst of 1999-2000 and, most dramatically, the 9/11 attacks. In quick succession, these events shook the industry and highlighted the need for change. Furthermore, as the millennium turned, a spate of kidnappings, hostage-takings, financial crises, corporate scandals, and political turmoils have elevated the risk level across the global economy.

With this increase in risk, so has the cost of insuring against it. That is indeed the picture drawn by contributors to this latest volume in occasional publications of the World Bank and edited by Theodore Moran.

---

[1] One contributor provides the most detailed definition of the PRI industry: the industry provides "financial risk solutions, such as credit risk transfers, asset-value guarantees, revenue guarantees, trade credit insurance, and the financing or transfer of mass tort liabilities" (p. 53).

In an interesting appendix that might have been even more compelling if woven into the text, Gerald West, a leader at the Multilateral Guaranty Agency (MIGA), puts it quite succinctly when he points to market uncertainty and its impact on the PRI market in the post-9/11 world and its influence on PRI. He shows that market uncertainty eroded the confidence of PRI providers, causing deterioration in the industry. West reports that the number of countries in which PRI was available declined in 2002/03, – pointing specifically to limited underwriting available in Turkey, Brazil, Mexico, and the Dominican Republic. He notes that "some investors were having difficulty obtaining coverage in China and Russia" (p. 197). Consequently, the PRI industry had deteriorated "from a dynamic and flexible marketplace to a harder and more cautious shadow of itself" (p. 203).

Based on a 2002 MIGA-Georgetown University symposium, this book is very timely and useful to policy makers and students of political risk, given the turbulent events of the recent past. The first two parts of the book address the insurance industry's perspective, taken from both the supply and demand sides of PRI, in that order.

In Part One, the book provides the industry supply side perspective, focusing on a public insurance provider (Berne Union), a London underwriter's analysis of Argentina, a New York insurer (AIG) on post-9/11 trade credit, and a risk consulting service. Several essays deal with 9/11, including one by John J. Salinger of AIG and another by Brian Duperreault of ACE Limited.

Julie A. Martin provides an innovative analysis of post-9/11 terrorism insurance, describing the PRI industry's excess underwriting capacity (p. 53), changes in the "terrorism market" (insurance rates for stand-alone terrorism coverage), and the emergence of a "stand-alone terrorism market" (p. 58) in the context of the Terrorism Risk Insurance Act of 2002. The latter is "a federal backstop for the terrorism market", which, administered by the United States Treasury Department, "backs insurers for certain losses arising from terrorism and is capped at $100 billion (p. 59).

The book not only provides a broad brush portrait of the PRI market in this age of uncertainty, but also introduces the reader to many useful concepts. For example, in Part Two of the book, from the supply side of PRI, Kenneth W. Hansen, the architect of a unique foreign exchange protection policy called "standby foreign exchange liquidity facility", describes how this innovative risk insurance policy can benefit companies involved in infrastrucuridal projects with long gestation period. Later, that same author refers to Argentina's "pesification" policy (p. 94), which, though he does not define it, was the forced conversion of dollar-denominated deposits into Argentinean pesos in early 2002. It also gives informative examples of the tensions or even contradictions between the reality on the ground and stated government policies or industry practices.

Likewise, Hansen discusses how Enron's infamous Dabhol Power Project, "the largest independent power project in the emerging markets", degenerated into "one of its largest financial and legal messes" (p. 93).

Part Three deals with finding common ground between supply and demand sides of PRI. Essays by industry insiders are particularly enlightening. Charles Berry, for instance, goes into some detail about the three key risks: inconvertibility, expropriation and political risk. David Bailey and Edith P. Quintrell, on the other hand, give private and public perspectives on the industry. The latter, an official at the Overseas Private Investment Corporation providing the public insurers' perspective, elaborates nicely on the gap between the neat categorization of political risk as defined and provided by PRI suppliers - expropriation, inconvertibility and political violence, and the reality on the ground, where the distinction between them is often blurred by circumstances (p. 177).

On the likely future of this industry, West speculates that, short of a strategic partnership between private and public risk insurance agencies, a Darwinian process of "natural selection" may result in a winnowing of the industry (p. 204).

This book sheds new light on the PRI industry, both from the demand as well as the supply side. Whereas the industry reaches into developing countries from the developed countries, readers in the former should be fascinated by the exposé of the inner workings of this industry. Kenneth W. Hansen's description of how the insurance industry has helped TNCs in breach of contract cases in infrastructure projects is an excellent case in point. Similarly, Anne H. Predieri and Audry Zuck inquire into whether PRI can serve as Penicillin to the ailing industry in this "gloomy economic climate that has been exacerbated by behaviors intended to maximize shareholder value" (p. 101).

Moran's extensive introductions to each part help smooth the unavoidable inconsistencies from which any edited volume is likely to suffer. He provides an excellent roadmap to the book, extracting the key points. Regrettably, the book deals solely with the insurance industry in the home countries of insurers. It would have been doubly useful if it could have brought in host country views from such emerging markets as Brazil, Indonesia, the Republic of Korea, Malaysia, Mexico, Thailand or Venezuela. Nevertheless, the book is critical reading for home and host countries, investors, and insurance companies and organizations providing PRI.

Tagi Sagafi-nejad
Texas A&M International University
United States

International Institutions and Multinational Enterprises

John-ren Chen, editor
(Cheltenham, Glos., Edward Elgar, 2004), 226 pages

This book is the result of a conference on the title theme at the University of Innsbruck in 2002. The papers contained in this volume cover a variety of subjects that mostly relate transnational corporations (TNCs) to government policies and social issues. They range from new empirical studies of labour issues related to TNCs to broad essays on issues such as corporate governance and TNCs' moral responsibility. There is not a clear line of reasoning or focus of the package of papers, though they all loosely relate to the issue of TNCs and their role/impact in the twenty-first century.

The papers are of varying quality, where quality is measured as contribution to conceptual thinking or to empirical knowledge. The study by Matthias Busse on "Multinational enterprises, core labour standards and the role of international institutions" (chapter six) is clearly the outstanding paper of the group. This is one of the empirical papers, but it also provides a clear and logical perspective on what key labour standards are, how they relate to foreign direct investment (FDI) and how governments and international organizations could act to improve the treatment of labour by domestic and international firms. Busse shows that four kinds of labour standards can be identified, and that for each of them, greater achievement of the standard correlates positively with the amount of FDI entering a country. This is a useful finding since it indicates that TNCs do not seem to be engaged in a "race to the bottom" to reduce costs by pursuing lower labour standards. Interestingly, the level of participation of a country in international agreements on labour standards was not correlated with either FDI or performance under those standards.

John Dunning's paper on moral aspects of TNC behaviour is illustrative of the difficulties in the book. His topic is certainly important in the context of trying to establish international institutional frameworks to guide TNCs into behaviour that serves welfare-increasing ends. The discussion in the essay is interesting and well-informed, but it does not lead to any particular conclusions about policy or about TNC behaviour. The idea that the market economy is very efficient at producing wealth does not raise many questions. The subsequent assertion that the market does not produce public goods well is a tantalizing argument that begs the question of how best to pursue such goals/produce such goods. Dunning raises a very useful point here but does not offer a satisfying direction to solve the problem.

The most difficult problem with the paper, however, is that Dunning does not present an analytical perspective on the issue of morals and TNCs. Other than recognizing that it is desirable for firms to operate in some sense "ethically", the paper does not suggest any direction to go towards identifying specific ethical behaviour that might be agreed globally, and then pursued in a policy context. It reminds me of the common response of business school to this issue: they wring their hands and assert that ethical decision-making matters – but then the curriculum content does not go beyond the assertion. Dunning is certainly in good company with those who have not discovered a way to deal with this issue, but I would have expected him to present some kind of framework for thinking about the problem, which is lacking here. He does, even so, suggest a variety of perspectives about moral issues, ranking absolute and relative morals, and proposing that church leaders look for moral common ground. So it would be unfair to criticize him for failing to make the effort. It is just discouraging to see that we are still floundering when it comes to structured thinking about what constitutes ethical decision-making for TNCs and, similarly, what defines corporate social responsibility of these firms.

Oliver Budzinski's essay on the International Competition Network is one of the essays that does focus specifically on TNCs and international institutions. The paper describes this newly-established international organization that groups the anti-trust authorities of several dozen countries toward the goal "to think broadly about international competition in the context of economic globalization and focused on issues like multi-jurisdictional merger review, the interface between trade and competition, and the future direction for cooperation between antitrust agencies". The author tries to establish some conceptual bases for thinking about the possible ways that this organization could have success in producing multi-country anti-trust rules, considering the different institutional goals of the participants. It is a very interesting, though not conclusive, exercise in examining a new international organization that is aimed at dealing with some of the issues raised by the existence and power of TNCs.

Two of the essays treat the subject of corporate governance, linking the question of good corporate governance to the pursuit of activities that are consistent with societal goals. The ideas presented, especially in the essay by Hans H. Hinterhuber, Kurt Matzler, Harald Pechlaner and Birgit Renzl, are interesting but unfocused. There is an enormous literature on this subject from the past ten years or so, and the authors do not build helpfully on it. The question of managing companies to meet stakeholder interests, including those of the international community, has been raised many times, and the literature shows a number of clear arguments about goals and methods to pursue them. The fact that an increasing number of countries are adopting pro-competition rules is pushing corporate governance to reflect a shareholder orientation more – with other stakeholders' interests pursued through legislative restrictions and subsidies. This is the logical way to deal with TNCs that may take actions that diverge from host-country interests or fail to deal with global concerns such as poverty or need for education. Even if the authors would disagree with this commentator, their arguments are not focused on a clear path towards understanding corporate governance and taking policy steps to re-orient it towards better compliance with societal goals.

All in all, this volume provides a handful of interesting ideas, but it does not deliver a clear message. The essays by Busse, Dunning, Budzinski, and Hinterhuber *et al.* have creative and interesting contents, so those certainly can be recommended for readers interested in thinking more about the relationship between international institutions and transnational corporations.

Robert E. Grosse
Thunderbird Associate Director
Glendale AZ
United States

India in the Global Software Industry: Innovations, Firm Strategies and Development

Anthony P. D'Costa and Eswaran Sridharan, editors
(London, Palgrave Macmillan, 2004), 278 pages

The Indian software industry is fast becoming a folklore of the modern day information technology (IT) revolution, and it is considered as an example *par excellence* of a technology-intensive industry establishing itself in a developing country. India has, indeed, caught many by surprise, and the progress is sometimes received with a mixed reaction. I once commented to an MBA class that the London underground was run by software written in India. Then came quick reply from one of the students: "that's why the trains are always late!" I am not sure if the Indians should take part of the blame for tube delays, but, for sure, they have proved how a little freedom in the domestic business environment and liberalization of trade regulations can go a long way in developing an industry that, not very long ago, hardly existed. No doubt that the industry has done all the Indians proud, but huge challenges lie ahead.

Because they provide an objective view of the situation, books like this volume are welcome additions to the growing literature on the subject. This, in particular, is a timely book that contains articles written by academics. Divorced from the business, but still interacting with it via their research projects, the authors are well placed to take stock of the situation objectively and suggest recommendations.

There are a total of eleven chapters in the book. The book takes a holistic approach by examining the firm, national and global level determinants of the industry's growth. Firm level determinants consist of innovatory capacities, cross-cultural issues and linkages of various kinds. National level issues consist of the role played by the state and federal governments in providing a helping hand to the industry through, for example, infrastructure development. Global level issues consist of the dynamics generated in the industry by the ever-changing demands of the consumer and the industry.

Chapter one highlights that the Indian software industry, though successful, still faces major hurdles, as it is still small in terms of its global market share and producing low value-added products, while its own domestic market is only one-third of the size of its export market. As remedies, the author recommends large scale investment in IT infrastructure, both physical and human, fostering R&D and entrepreneurial skills, and forming close partnership with transnational corporations (TNCs).

Chapter two introduces the determinants of innovation in the case of the Indian IT industry and also provides the gist of innovation-related issues dealt in the book. Can India follow the examples of the Republic of Korea and Taiwan Province of China where firms started as assemblers of semiconductors for TNCs but moved up the value chain with the help of investment in research and development (R&D)? In order to be able to take a similar path, the industry needs to diversify and, in this regard, it should take advantage of "return entrepreneurs" from Silicon Valley. Business-friendly government legislations and improved infrastructure would also be needed. R&D in India has historically been the domain of public institutions and TNCs – the latter have shown added interests in IT recently, given the highly-skilled cost-effective labour force available in the country.

The message contained in chapter three (partly based on a survey) is that the Indian software industry is locked into the low-end of the software market, supplying mostly to the United States market. This lock-in effect has hindered its development of innovative capacity, which the industry must foster in order to move up in the value chain. This, according to author, can be done by diversifying both the geographic and the customer base and by establishing linkages with the domestic market alongside export markets. It is emphasized that face-to-face interaction with the end-users can be pivotal in enhancing key tacit skills and exploring new business opportunities.

Chapter four attempts to understand the role of governmental measures in enhancing innovation-based competitive advantage of the software firms. An econometric model is used to determine the variables that govern the innovative performance of firms. The descriptive and analytical findings in this chapter show the importance of State measures in the present-day success of the IT sector. It is a good reminder that, in a bureaucracy-ridden country such as India, a series of State initiatives have played an important role in the development of the present day IT sector. Lest it be forgotten, hidden behind these State measures are those technocrats who had an early vision of the growth path the industry could take with help from the State. The authors urge further tapping into the resources not-resident Indians offer, and increased focus on the domestic market for the development of the industry. Fortunately, the tenth five-year plan makes some important provisions in this direction, e.g. IT applications in the energy and the railways sectors. The multiple regression model used to assess the determinants of innovative performance shows that export intensity has no bearing upon the innovativeness; among firm-specific variables, size, selling cost, and skill intensity are found to be statistically significant variables.

Chapter five, written by researchers from Israel, provides an interesting commentary on the Indian IT industry from an Israeli perspective. The chapter is descriptive in nature, and it compares and contrasts the Israeli experience of developing its IT sector with India's and offers some useful insights, some of which are drawn after interviews with three cross-sectionally selected Indian companies (Wipro, Sasken, Hughes). Their most pertinent observation and suggestion seem to be on the support for start-up firms with regard to venture capital and R&D.

Chapter six addresses the issue of product development, which is one of the proffered solutions for Indian companies seeking to come out of their low-end service businesses. A case study approach is adopted to understand the intricacies of product development business. The difficulties associated with successful product development are easy to understand. Whereas the market for service software is the client's domain, the market for product development has to be found, developed and nurtured. As the authors put it succinctly: "product development requires discipline: in analysis, decision-making, and implementation. It involves intuitive understanding of markets, users and their needs combined with creative problem-solving, elegant design and robust architecture" (p. 159). The deepening of the domestic market for software products, collaboration between large and small firms, and checks on software piracy could be building blocks of successful product development.

Chapter seven is a lucid and candid account of what is missing for the further development of the IT industry in India that ought to be read by all those connected with the industry, in particular, government officials. The author provides a short but fascinating account of China's growing supremacy in the IT sector, both software and hardware, and also offers a valuable policy prescription for prospective entrepreneurs and public officials. The author's suggested remedies include: a greater interface of IT scholars with Silicon Valley; well-meaning and concerted efforts by the Government to rout out the corrupt and inept elements in government machinery; an overall improvement in the infrastructure; and incentives to motivate Indian talent to return to India. Also, no less important is the author's emphasis on the need for diversifying into the hardware side of the industry and into product development both for the domestic and overseas markets.

Chapter eight re-emphasizes the point that linkages help organizations build technological capabilities. The descriptive analysis is based on the links Nortel, the Canadian telecommunications firm, formed with Indian and Chinese partners. The lesson seems to be that learning from alliances should carry a *strategic intent*: i.e. a conscious effort to learn from different projects should exist. In addition, the involvement of the academia in technology networks can create significant positive spillovers. The Indian telecommunications industry is slowly emerging from State controls, which, in itself, given the vastness of the country and ample opportunities it provides, should accelerate the pace of collaborative activities for the benefits of the business and the non-business world.

Chapter nine addresses the issue of innovation and entrepreneurship in the context of the software industry in India. There is an enormous amount of theoretical and applied literature on both of these topics, and it is understandable if only a part of it is captured here. The central hypothesis is that, in order for Indian firms to move up the value chain, they need entrepreneurs who have foresight and vision, and can take calculated risks. In turn, the budding entrepreneurs need to be supported by active venture capital and reliable infrastructure. The chapter is primarily based on interviews with 16 entrepreneurs. Among the findings is the fact that most entrepreneurs in the software industry come from middle class backgrounds and only a few have a business background. Interestingly, most did not find the Indian market encouraging, which is a little bit surprising given the Indian market's vast potentials.

Chapter ten charts the growth of two well-known firms in the IT business, Infosys and NIIT. The underlying theme in the successful growth of these firms is the vision of the entrepreneurs who founded them. In particular, the learning traits of both organizations stand out. The IT business is human capital intensive; it is the people who drive the business forward unlike manufacturing where the physical operation of machinery is equally important. Both firms have successfully harnessed their human resources and channelled their energies in the right directions.

So what lessons do the discussions in the book lead to? Some of the key points are: IT firms need to be innovative, focus on the domestic market, move up the value chain, and form alliances with overseas firms with the intent of learning. In addition, technocrats in government need to become more imaginative in attracting entrepreneurs into the IT sector. There is a lot that can be learnt from China in this respect.

This is a timely and densely written book. Although it does not break any new theoretical grounds, it does successfully draw attention to pertinent issues facing the present day Indian IT industry. The highly descriptive presentations at places could have been tightened, and conclusions of some chapters could be shorter. A section on the central and state government policies that helped the IT industry grow could have been added. All in all, this is a well thought-out book that would be interesting to a cross-section of business and academic practitioners.

Satwinder Singh
Department of International Business Studies
Witan International College
Reading, United Kingdom.

World Investment Report 2004:
The Shift Towards Services

(New York and Geneva, United Nations, 2004),
xxx+436 pages

Foreign direct investment (FDI) is increasingly recognized, mainly since the 1980s, as a vital force in fostering long-term economic development. In addition to injecting capital, FDI has the much desired potential to create jobs, transfer technology (including management skills), enhance export capacity and raise productivity. The possible disadvantages of FDI or the possible conflict between transnational corporations (TNCs) and nation-states seem to have been forgotten or assumed to be controllable. Governments are competing among themselves to attract FDI by taking measures to improve the investment climate, such as reducing investment and trade restrictions and offering more incentives. To be sure, it is claimed that Governments in Latin America, for example, conceded too much to foreign private investors when they privatized public utilities. Complaints on abuses of monopoly power or excessive incentives incompatible with possible benefits are sometimes heard. Nevertheless, FDI is deemed as essential for the competitiveness of nations. The risks to the domestic economy or to the political, social and cultural fabric of the host countries are often ignored. Most researchers seem to agree that the benefit of FDI exceeds costs (Oxelheim and Ghauri, 2004, p. 10).

The World Investment Report 2004 includes, as one has learnt to expect, a wealth of interesting information and data. As in other such reports, the first part (chapters one and two) traces changes in the stocks and flows of FDI, including regional trends. Part Two discusses the shift of FDI towards services and the accelerated pace of the offshoring of corporate service functions. It examines the trends and analyzes the opportunities as well as the challenges that arise from these developments. Part Three examines national and international policy challenges. The *Report* includes 72 boxes with specific – sometimes anecdotal – information on many topics, ranging from a list of the 50 largest TNCs from developing countries to a description of the rise and spread of retail TNCs to the GATS and subsidies. In addition, the *WIR04* includes more than 150 tables and figures as well as a detailed and eye-opening statistical annex.

Part One presents figures on the trends and regional as well as sectoral distribution of FDI. It contains quite an optimistic outlook of FDI recovery after the major decline reported in 2003. Prospects are said to be particularly bright for services and for the relocation of a wide range of corporate functions. It reports that there are, at least, 61,000 TNCs with over 900,000 foreign affiliates. These affiliates account for one-tenth of the world GDP and one third of world's exports, and their shares are increasing. The degree of transnationality of countries has also continued to rise. International production has been quite concentrated, but much less so than a decade ago. The 100 largest TNCs accounted for 12 % of assets, 13% of employment and 14% of sales by all foreign affiliates compared with 21%, 21% and 27%, respectively, in 1990. In terms of the geographic spread, the most transnational of the TNCs is one only a few scholars would recognize as an obvious candidate, the Deutsche Post World Net with affiliates in 97 countries.

The *WIR04* notes the increasing importance of outward FDI from developing countries. The overseas expansion of TNCs from developing countries is growing at a fast rate. From a negligible share in 1990, outward FDI from developing countries has increased to account for over one-tenth of the world's total stock and 6% of the world total flows in 2003. Indeed, firms in these countries have learnt that to survive and flourish in a globalized world, they must be competitive internationally, which necessitates operating across national boundaries and holding a portfolio of assets in different locations.

As in the previous editions, the *Report* also presents several indices, aimed at capturing different phenomena related to FDI. Thus, the Inward Performance Index gauges the attractiveness of a country to FDI. The potential to attract FDI is measured by an Inward FDI Potential Index. The Transnationality Index is an attempt to measure the degree of transnationality of firms. *WIR04* presents for the first time a new index – the Outward FDI Performance Index – measured as the ratio of a country's share in world outward FDI flows to its share in world GDP. The leaders on this index are Belgium and Singapore, but also Luxembourg and Panama, because of transshipped FDI.

Statistics on the outflows of FDI places the United States in the first place, followed by Luxembourg, France and the United Kingdom, in this order. The high ranking of Luxembourg is a result of transshipped FDI. Both Panama and Luxembourg are at the top of the list of countries in terms of the Performance Index – mainly because these countries are used as tax havens. Hong Kong is another illustration. The territory is a top recipient of FDI inflows ($13.6 billion in 2003). It is also the seventh largest outward foreign direct investor and the largest among developing countries. More than a half of the outward FDI stock were to four tax havens, and round-tripping FDI from China through Hong Kong (China) and back was estimated at about 25% of outward FDI flows.

Statistics on FDI are based on information collected by UNCTAD, mostly from the individual countries, the International Monetary Fund and the Organisation for Economic Co-operation and Development. These sources are the best available, but are not free from limitations. The coverage of the data in different countries varies considerably. Thus, in the case of business services, some countries include the value of the real estate itself, not only the services of real estate agents. Hong Kong (China) and other economies include holding companies, which greatly inflate the value of FDI. Furthermore, to date, each country within the European Union is considered an independent entity. Therefore, an investment by an Irish airline in Belgium is considered FDI, even though the EU created one European Common Aviation Area, transforming intra-community air service from international to domestic.

UNCTAD defines a TNC as a parent enterprise and its foreign affiliates. A threshold of 10% of equity is considered sufficient. Under this definition, Canadian National Railway Company is one of the world's 100 largest non-financial TNCs, although it operates only in two host countries. Raymond Vernon, in his studies, required operations in six countries for a firm to be classified as a TNC.

I could not find in *WIR04* an explicit definition of the term "global industry". The *Report* refers to the telecommunications industry as an emerging global industry because of the dramatic increase in inward FDI. Michael Porter defines a global industry as one in which "rivals compete against each other on a truly worldwide basis" (Porter, 1990, p. 54). When competition in each country is essentially independent, the industry is *multi-domestic.* Under this definition, neither telecoms nor water nor electricity supply is a global industry. In professional business services, there are a small number of giant networks, e.g. the Big Four in accounting competing with each other on a worldwide or, at least, regional basis. But there are also thousands of small firms operating domestically. Is the industry global? Some segments are – others are not. Again, definitions are non-trivial!

The definition of FDI is based on the balance of payments statistics. Thus, non-equity forms of FDI, such as sub-contracting, management contracts, turnkey arrangements, franchising, licensing and product sharing, are reflected only as receipts of royalty and management fees. In many services, non-equity forms are much more important than equity investment. To be sure, these limitations and others are all pointed out in the *Report*. Researchers using the data are well advised to read carefully the definitions in annex B of *WIR04*.

There are many regional differences, noted in chapter two. Outflows from the United States zoomed and resulted in a negative net balance in FDI flows of $122 billion – the highest deficit ever. *WIR04* is silent on the prospects of a plunge in the dollar or revaluation of Asian currencies and the probable impact of such shifts on FDI flows.

Part Two of the *Report* analyses the growth of FDI in services and its economic impact – less so other implications, e.g. for international business theory. It notes a major shift in the composition of FDI. In the early 1970s, services accounted for about a quarter of the FDI stock. In 1990, the primary sector accounted for 9% of the world FDI stock, manufacturing for 42% and services for 49%. In 2002, the primary sector declined to 6%, manufacturing to 34% and services rose to about 60% of the world FDI stock. Between 1990 and 2002, the global stock of both inward and outward FDI in the primary sector more than doubled. During the same period, FDI in manufacturing rose three times while FDI in services more than quadrupled. Outward FDI in services, which were previously almost entirely from the United States, came also from the EU and Japan, and the share of developing countries climbed rapidly from 1% in 1990 to 10% in 2002.

The composition of FDI in services also saw a dramatic change. In 1990, 65% of the inward stock in services was in trade and finance. By 2002, the share of these two industries dropped to 47%. During the same period, a rapid expansion in FDI was noted in electricity, communication, postal services and water supply – all public utilities that were privatized and became open to foreign investors. Large increases were registered also in business services and in education. More recently, certain health services also became transnational. The value of the FDI stock in electric power generation and distribution increased 14-fold. In telecoms, storage and transport, the stock increased 16-fold and in business services, 9-fold. This major shift, the *Report* points out, came because countries had liberalized their service FDI regimes and privatized public utilities. Unlike manufacturing, and despite the increased cross-border tradability of information-intensive services, the integrated production of services is still in its embryonic stage. Thus, 84% of sales of services by foreign affiliates of United States TNCs in 2001 were local sales in host countries compared to 61% in goods.

Services comprised, in 2001, 72% of the GDP in developed countries, 52% in developing and 57% in Central and East European (CEE) countries. Based on this indicator, *WIR04* notes that there is a room for a vast increase in the share of service FDI. Today, international production networks in services are in their infancy, and services TNCs are significantly less transnationalized than their manufacturing counterparts (20% compared to 40%, according to United States data quoted in the *Report*). Yet, services are known to be less tradable, and certain services, e.g. security and other government services, media, health or education, may always be domestic for political, cultural or social reasons.

Moreover, there are two major reasons to believe that the statistics on services FDI underestimate the real size of this phenomenon. First, a large percentage of the services is embedded in goods. These services are not counted in official statistics as services, but as goods (usually manufacturing). Yet, much of the ownership specific advantages of manufacturing TNCs are based on design, computer technology and marketing efforts. The more complex the operation of a good, the higher the service component in it and the greater the probability that consumers buy a product based both on pre-production services such as market research or R&D and specific post-sales services (e.g. maintenance contract) that are deemed indispensable. These service functions are presented in the national statistics as a part of the production of goods. Only when the service functions are outsourced to a service organization they are counted as services.

Second, in several service industries, non-equity forms prevail rather than FDI. In the hotel industry, for example, it is a common practice for hotel operators to enter into management contracts without ownership of the real estate. The same is true in car rentals, restaurants, auditing, engineering, legal advice and other professional services. In all of these cases, the ownership advantage of firms is reflected in intangible assets such as reputation or organizational capabilities, information processing or managerial skills and knowledge (Aharoni, 2000). The physical assets are not owned by the TNCs. For very different reason, airlines are globalizers that are not allowed to globalize. (For details see Aharoni, 2002). Inward FDI in European airlines has been constrained by ownership requirements in bilateral Air Service Agreements. They therefore are forced to use code sharing and strategic alliances to augment international competitiveness. In all of these cases, FDI stock and flow data do not capture these activities. The magnitude of these two statistical biases is not easy to establish. Clearly, therefore, the size of the services sector is grossly underestimated in the official statistics.

WIR04 notes (endnote 7, p. 148) that "it is difficult to say whether the full liberalization of FDI would result in much higher FDI". It points out that in the hotel industry, most countries have lifted restrictions and seek not only the presence but also the capital investment of international hotel chains. My own research shows significant differences between the hotel and airline industries. As pointed out above, hotel chains achieve reputation by excellent management. These skills are different than those required to buy real estate. Airlines, too, do not have to own their planes – they can lease them. However, they must create – among other things – an efficient network. The Air Service Agreements prevent the use of a hub and spoke system, highly successful in the United States. The airlines industry is a global, mature and oligopolistic industry. One reason for its continued losses or low levels of returns on investment is the inability to reach economies of scale, of scope and mainly of network. If a guess may be offered, the liberalization of the airlines regime would result in a drastic consolidation through M&As (Aharoni, 2004). Certainly, one must study carefully the different key factors of success in each one of the extremely diverse industries shown under the banner "services".

Chapter four is devoted to the growing trend of offshoring of corporate service functions. Offshoring has experienced a drastic change. It is no longer confined to outsourcing of unskilled repetitive manufacturing work. Today, the codification of jobs and information technology allow offshoring of knowledge-intensive work, e.g. sophisticated computer development, blood testing, x-ray diagnosis and R&D. These new developments have caused increasing anxiety in the industrialized countries. It is claimed that no job is protected from an onslaught of competition from lower cost employees in India, China or CEE countries.

The *Report* distinguishes between captive offshoring and outsourcing. The first is executed within the network of a TNC. The latter is achieved by subcontracting to other firms. To date, a majority of offshoring is done by large TNCs, perhaps because of their competence in managing integrated operations; re-routing business operation offshore is a major undertaking that needs to be managed carefully. Most of offshoring operations are undertaken by the TNCs from the United States and the United Kingdom.

A concern about job losses triggered calls for protectionism. Lofty ideals of the need for economic liberalization are often forgotten when domestic interests are perceived as threatened and high-paid jobs are perceived as lost to lower wages countries. The *Report* lists, in chapter five, several attempts to limit offshoring by government agencies in developed countries or by private firms that currently receive government contracts. *WIR04* concludes that developed countries will learn to adapt and that the concerns are likely to be unfounded: "[t]he final outcome should again be a win-win situation for the parties involved" (p. 216). The *Report* offers a careful and dispassionate analysis of the benefits and costs of these new developments. The crusaders against "loss of jobs" would benefit from reading such an objective analysis and may also benefit from the recognition of the facts. *WIR04* points out (based on a McKinsey's study) that, in 2001, Ireland enjoyed the highest share of offshoring – a quarter of the world market (p. 147). Four largest recipients – Ireland, India, Canada, Israel – accounted for over 71% of offshoring, mostly in various information technology-enables services. To be sure, the share of developing countries and CEE is increasing and the geographic scope for location of service FDI is broadening. Yet, several studies, quoted mainly in chapter five, show that the impact on employment in the two developed countries accounting for 82% of offshoring – the United States and the United Kingdom – is minimal. Unfortunately, instead of recognizing the moves as a manifestation of a shift in comparative advantage, offshoring is sometimes presented as a zero-sum game resulting inevitably in job losses in developed countries

International agreements covering both goods and services FDI are proliferating at the bilateral, regional and multilateral levels. The national and international policy challenges are analysed in Part Three of the *Report* – following and updating the discussion of the 2003 edition of the *WIR*. This part also focuses on services. The *Report* takes a macro view of many issues. For example, it does not discuss how to find a "development-oriented balance". This is a challenge in any field, but much more so when services are discussed. Services are extremely heterogeneous, ranging over many diverse activities with different technologies and scope. The policy issues are poles apart, and their treatments cannot be the same for all types of services. Adding to these problems are the difficulties inherent in reaching a satisfactory legal definition of complex economic issues. Certainly, "strong, independent and regulatory structures are vital if the potential economic benefits of FDI are to be realized" (p. 141). The *Report* also stresses the need for maintaining flexibility (p. 236). This reviewer would add that it is essential to make sure that, if TNCs received incentives and concessions, these TNCs would deliver what was expected of them. Further, it is crucial to avoid costly beggar-thy-neighbour policy wars, including downward pressures on labour and environmental standards (Oman, 2001).

All in all, this annual publication is an extensive survey of the determinants and the drivers of FDI as well as the political and legal regimes in which they take place. It has justifiably become an essential research tool for all those interested in FDI. It is also of great practical value to decision-makers in both governments and TNCs. It supplies so many intriguing data and so many fascinating facts that no summary can capture its richness. Researchers of international business should certainly read carefully the whole *Report*. It would have been easier to use this rich source of data if an index were added. Further, adding more references to scholarly work done outside the United Nations or other governmental organizations could enhance the hundreds of references presented in this publication.

Future publications might also include less ambiguous statements about the need to strike a development-oriented balance. This reviewer would like to see a careful analysis of the limits to globalization. One would hope that the *Report* would look at the links between private capital and governments, investigate the role of culture and examine the impact of technological changes. Future *Reports* should feel free to present views and assessments on the prospects for the future of TNCs and FDI. Furthermore, it would be nice to learn more on the reasons some industries are more global than others, why certain services become global while others lag behind and what the optimum balance between incentives to attract FDI and regulation to safeguard public interest is. Perhaps the *Report* could speculate about the impact of global integration on the possible reduction of differences in labour costs across countries as well as about the political, cultural and social dimensions of globalisation. Finally, it would be nice to see more attempts to offer facts, data and theories on the inner working of the TNCs and on the determinants of success of TNCs. This is a quite demanding wish list. Yet, high achievements of UNCTAD in the past allows one to expect that Organisation to meet even more difficult challenges.

Yair Aharoni
Professor Emeritus
Tel Aviv University
Israel

References

Aharoni, Yair (2000). "The role of reputation in global professional business services", in Yair Aharoni and Lilach Nachum, eds, *Globalization of Services: Some Implications for Theory and Practice* (London: Routledge), pp. 125-141.

_____ (2002). "The globalizer that cannot globalize: the world airline industry", mimeo. (http://www.aueb.gr/deos/EIBA2002.files/PAPERS/C214.pdf).

_____ (2004). "The race for FDI in services: the case of the airline industry", in Lars Oxelheim and Pervez Ghauri, eds., *European Union and the Race for Foreign Direct Investment in Europe* (Amsterdam: Elsevier), pp. 381-406.

Oxelheim, Lars and Pervez Ghauri (eds.) (2004). *European Union and the Race for Foreign Direct Investment in Europe (*Amsterdam: Elsevier).

Oman, C. (2001). *Policy Competition and Foreign Direct Investment (*Paris: OECD).

Porter, Michael (1990). *The Competitive Advantage of Nations* (New York: Free Press).

JUST PUBLISHED

International Investment Agreements: Key Issues
Volumes I, II and III
Sales No. E.05.II.D.6 (UNCTAD/ITE/IIT/2004/10)

The three volumes bring together the 27 booklets dealing with individual issues in international investment agreements. Together, they constitute the most comprehensive treatment of key issues in international investment agreements (IIAs) to date.

These booklets are combined in this three-volume compilation, each of them constituting a chapter. Each chapter deals with a specific issue, structured along the same lines, with particular attention to the development dimension of international rule making in its given area. Almost all chapters address a standard set of questions: How is the concept/issue in question defined? How has it been used in relevant instruments to date? What are its connections with other key issues? And what are the development implications? At the same time, consideration is given to the fact that it is up to States to decide which path to pursue, which framework to use and which policy to follow. Hence, the chapters do not contain recommendations as to the formulation, conceptualization or approach to use. Rather, each chapter outlines options available to negotiators tasked with drafting the respective treaty provisions, pointing to the specific circumstances that may or may not apply in the pursuit of each.

Competition

**UNCTAD Series on Issues in
International Investment Agreements**
Sales No.: E.04.II.D.44

This paper examines how competition issues have been addressed in IIAs and other relevant instruments dealing with international investment. The paper identifies three main issues that arise in this context: i.e. first, the types of anticompetitive practices or "restrictive business practices" that need to be considered; second procedural issues related to extraterritoriality and international cooperation in competition matters; and thirdly issues related to harmonization measures in this area, and discusses the different approaches to competition policy for economic development in individual countries. Finally, the paper considers the various options open to negotiators when drafting competition provisions.

State Contracts

UNCTAD Series on Issues in International Investment Agreements
Sales No.: E.05.II.D.5

State contracts have played a major role in the FDI process, especially in developing countries that are dependent upon the exploitation of natural resources for their economic welfare. Often, investment in a sector, such as petroleum, is open only to a State entity or through the making of a contract with the relevant State entity. In relation to IIAs, the issue of State contracts concerns the following: (a) the extension of investment agreements' protection to State contracts that is dependent on the scope of the definition of investment, the exclusion of certain State contracts from their coverage and in how far dispute settlement provisions of the agreements apply to State contracts; (b) the preservation of host country discretion in the negotiation, conclusion and regulation of State contracts which can be based on inscribing the basic principle of good faith and periodic review into an IIA; (c) the duties towards private investor parties to State contracts that compensate for the more favourable position of the State by allowing for clauses on stabilization, choice of law, arbitration and the breach of contract on the part of the host country government; and (d) the development of substantive regimes of State contracts in IIAs.

The REIO Exception in MFN Treatment Clauses
UNCTAD Series on International Investment
Policies for Development
Sales No.: E.05.II.D.1

This paper examines the issue of regional economic integration organization (REIO) exceptions in IIAs and its possible effects, in particular with regard to developing countries. A REIO exception excludes the applicability of the principle of most-favoured-nation treatment with regard to preferential treatment that members of a REIO grant other REIO members and their investors. While this clause appears indispensable for the pursuit of internal investment policies, including possible future integration measures, it might undermine the principle of non-discrimination as one of the essential rights in IIAs. Developing countries in particular may be concerned about the effects of such an exception upon their ability to benefit from membership of IIAs, particularly those that involve developed country members of a REIO.

International Investment Instruments: A Compendium, Volume XIII
(forthcoming)

Volume XIII is divided into the following three sections: Part One contains selected regional instruments; Part Two reproduces investment-related provisions in a number of bilateral agreements not covered in previous volumes. Part Three contains texts of prototype BITs not covered in previous volumes.

International Investment Instruments: A Compendium, Volume XIV
(forthcoming)

Volume XIV is divided into the following two sections: Part One reproduces investment-related provisions in selected bilateral agreements and a framework agreement not covered in previous volumes, Part Two contains the text of a prototype BIT not covered in previous volumes.

International Investment Disputes on the Rise
UNCTAD/WEB/ITE/IIT/2004/2 (Occasional Note)

This note documents the recent increase in international investment disputes arising from investment agreements. The cases cover a wide range of economic activities and various types of foreign involvement, and relate to key provisions in investment agreements. These developments raise a number of systemic and substantive issues and have serious development implications.

Progress Report: Work Undertaken within UNCTAD's Work Programme on International Investment Agreements in 2004
UNCTAD/IIT/ITE/2004/Misc.15/Rev.1

The report provides an overview of the activities undertaken within the IIA work programme in 2004. it mainly reports on the policy analysis and research work undertaken and the technical assistance and capacity-building activities organized. It also provides a summary assessment of the impact of this work.

Disclosure of the Impact of Corporations on Society
Sales No. E.04.II.D.18 (UNCTAD/ITE/TEB/2003/7)

This publication gives an overview of the current trends and issues in corporate social responsibility (CSR) reporting. The Secretariat's report on the disclosure of the impact of corporations on society is contained in Part I. Part II includes the proceedings of a one-day workshop organized immediately after the 20th session for the members of ISAR interested in this issue. The publication addresses a number of CSR issues, such as the drivers of the phenomenon of corporate social responsibility, major reporting initiatives, the benefits of CSR for corporations as well as for the sustainable development of countries and also how the accounting profession and standard-setters can respond to the current situation in order to develop a harmonized social reporting model that takes into account stakeholders' needs and cost-benefit consideration of corporate reporting.

Investment Policy Review of Benin
UNCTAD/ITE/IPC/2004/11

The demise of social economic policies in 1989, characterized by widespread privatization policies and sweeping political reforms, were crucial in enabling Benin to attract FDI. However, in 1994 Benin experienced a dramatic drop in FDI from which it has yet to recover. The positive spillovers from FDI (contribution to employment, technology transfer and trade diversification) continue to be limited, with further scope for improvement. The IPR of Benin analyzes three main areas that should contribute to increasing the efficiency and effectiveness of FDI. Firstly, the legislative framework of Benin that, initially, contributed to increasing FDI needs to be further modernized and the governance structure improved. Secondly, the review identifies four sectors, agriculture and agro-industry, tourism, cotton, and mining, in which Benin enjoys a comparative advantage. These should be further exploited in order to improve the attractiveness of Benin FDI recipient. Thirdly, the port of Cotonou will continue to play a vital role in the nation's development process. By improving the infrastructure and by rationalizing its functioning, the port will consolidate its position as a major regional hub and should contribute to attracting more export orientated FDI.

India's Outward FDI: A Giant Awakening?
UNCTAD/DITE/IIAB/2004/1 (Occasional Note)

This note provides a detailed analysis of the destination, sectoral distribution, drivers, regulatory framework and outlook of India's outward FDI. It concludes that Indian outward FDI is expected to grow, in particular in information technology and software services. India's membership in various regional integration arrangements also provides Indian firms with a favourable platform to strengthen their presence in these partner economies. Not least, the encouragement and the significant liberalization of policies by the Government of India will continue to play an instrumental role in the expansion of Indian firms abroad.

Outward FDI From Brazil: Poised for Take-Off?
UNCTAD/WEB/ITE/IIA/2004/16

This note analyzes FDI outflows from Brazil and shows in particular that most of the country's FDI stock is located in tax-haven economies, suggesting that financial motivations have played a major role in its outward FDI. It provides an outlook of Brazil's outward FDI suggesting that investment abroad by Brazilian TNCs appears poised to take off.

UNCTAD Investment Brief: FDI in services: a growing business for EPZs
UNCTAD/WEB/ITE/IIA/2004/17

Export processing zones (EPZs) have traditionally been associated with exports of goods, such as garments and electronics. Service activities have mostly been limited to warehousing and trade facilitation. New research shows that EPZs now often target a broader range of services, many requiring advanced skills. While EPZs can be effective in attracting FDI, the challenge is to ensure that benefits extend beyond their fences.

Investment brief: what services do IPAs target?

UNCTAD research shows that investment promotion agencies increasingly target investment in services. Computer services, tourism and call centres are the most actively promoted areas in terms of FDI. The first UNCTAD Investment Brief, drawing on an UNCTAD survey of 61 national IPAs in 2004, highlights various aspects of the emerging shift towards services in the field of FDI.

Press materials on FDI issued in November 2004 to February 2005
(Please visit http://www.unctad.org/press for details)

Title	Date	Document symbol
KYOTO PROTOCOL OFFERS INVESTMENT OPPORTUNITIES IN DEVELOPING COUNTRIES	15/02/05	UNCTAD/PRESS/PR/2005/010
CHINA SET TO STAY GROWTH COURSE: UNCTAD HANDBOOK OF STATISTICS 2004	28/01/05	UNCTAD/PRESS/PR/2005/007
WORLD ECONOMIC SITUATION AND PROSPECTS 2005	25/01/05	UNCTAD/PRESS/EB/2005/001
NEW ROLE FOR JAPAN'S SOGO SHOSHA AS THEY SHIFT FROM MANUFACTURING TO SERVICES	20/01/05	UNCTAD/PRESS/IN/2005/002
NEW ISSUE OF TRANSNATIONAL CORPORATIONS JOURNAL PUBLISHED	14/01/05	UNCTAD/PRESS/IN/2005/001
WORLD FDI FLOWS GREW AN ESTIMATED 6% IN 2004, ENDING DOWNTURN	11/01/05	UNCTAD/PRESS/PR/2005/002
OUTWARD FDI FROM BRAZIL: POISED FOR TAKE-OFF?	08/12/04	UNCTAD/PRESS/EB/2004/014
INTERNATIONAL INVESTMENT DISPUTES ON THE RISE	29/11/04	UNCTAD/PRESS/EB/2004/013
SOUTH-SOUTH INVESTMENT AGREEMENTS PROLIFERATING	23/11/04	UNCTAD/PRESS/PR/2004/036
UNCTAD PUBLISHES FORECASTING STUDY ON FDI	10/11/04	UNCTAD/PRESS/EB/2004/011
INVESTMENT AGENCIES TARGET FDI IN SERVICES	02/11/04	UNCTAD/PRESS/EB/2004/010
EXPERTS STRESS IMPORTANCE OF GOOD GOVERNANCE IN ATTRACTING FOREIGN INVESTMENT	01/11/04	UNCTAD/PRESS/IN/2004/020

Books received since December 2004

Brink, Charlotte H., *Measuring Political Risk : Risks to Foreign Investment* (Aldershot, Hants: Ashgate, 2004), vii+200 pages.

Bernanke, Ben S. and Michael Woodford, eds., *The Inflation-Targeting Debate* (Chicago: University of Chicago Press, 2005), 432 pages.

Chen, John-ren, ed., *International Institutions and Multinational Enterprises: Global Players - Global Markets* (Cheltenham, Glos.: Edward Elgar, 2004), 226 pages.

Eichengreen, Barry and Ricardo Hausmann, eds., *Other People's Money: Debt Denomination and Financial Instability in Emerging Market Economies* (Chicago: University of Chicago Press, 2005), vii+296 pages.

Estrin, Saul and Klaus E. Meyer, eds., *Investment Strategies In Emerging Markets* (Cheltenham, Glos.: Edward Elgar, 2004), 384 pages.

Forssbæck, Jens and Lars Oxelheim, *Money Markets And Politics: A Study of European Financial Integration and Monetary Policy Options* (Cheltenham, Glos.: Edward Elgar, 2004), 302 pages.

Kim, Wan-Soon and Michael Jae Choo, *Managing the Road to Globalisation: the Korean Experience* (Seoul: Korea Trade-Investment Promotion Agency, 2002), 271 pages.

Liang, Guoyong, *New Competition: Foreign Direct Investment and Industrial Development in China* (Rotterdam: Erasmus Research Institute of Management, 2004), xiii+385 pages.

Navaretti, Giorgio Barba and Venables, Anthony J., *Multinational Firms in the World Economy* (Princeton, NJ: Princeton University Press, 2004), xiii+325 pages.

Wei, Yingqi Annie and V.N. Balasubramnyam, eds, *Foreign Direct Investment: Six Country Case Studies* (Cheltenham, Glos.: Edward Elgar, 2004), xvii+218 pages.

Zarsky, Lyuba, ed. *International Investment for Sustainable Development: Balancing Rights and Rewards* (London: Earthscan, 2005), xiv+225 pages.

Submission statistics

Figure 1. *Transnational Corporations*: breakdown of manuscripts as of 31 December 2004

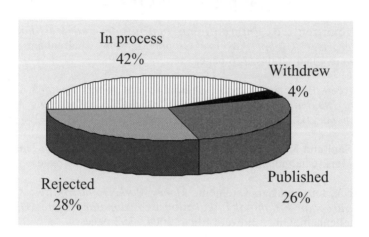

Figure 2. *Transnational Corporations*: breakdown of manuscripts since inception

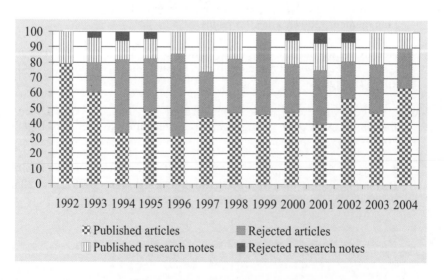

GUIDELINES FOR CONTRIBUTORS

I. Manuscript preparation

Authors are requested to submit three (3) copies of their manuscript in English, with a signed statement that the text (or parts thereof) has not been published or submitted for publication elsewhere, to:

> The Editor, *Transnational Corporations*
> UNCTAD
> Division on Investment, Technology
> and Enterprise Development
> Room E-10054
> Palais des Nations
> CH-1211 Geneva 10
> Switzerland
> Tel: (41) 22 907 5707
> Fax: (41) 22 907 0498
> E-mail: Karl.Sauvant@UNCTAD.org

Articles should, normally, not exceed 30 double-spaced pages (12,000 words). All articles should have an abstract not exceeding 150 words. Research notes should be between 10 and 15 double-spaced pages. Book reviews should be around 1,500 words, unless they are review essays, in which case they may be the length of an article. Footnotes should be placed at the bottom of the page they refer to. An alphabetical list of references should appear at the end of the manuscript. Appendices, tables and figures should be on separate sheets of paper and placed at the end of the manuscript.

Manuscripts should be word-processed (or typewritten) and double-spaced (including references) with wide margins. Pages should be numbered consecutively. The first page of the manuscript should contain: (i) title; (ii) name(s) and institutional affiliation(s) of the author(s); and (iii) mailing address, e-mail address, telephone and facsimile numbers of the author (or primary author, if more than one).

Authors should provide a diskette of manuscripts only when accepted for publication. The diskette should be labelled with the title of the article, the name(s) of the author(s) and the software used (e.g. WordPerfect, Microsoft Word, etc.).

Transnational Corporations has the copyright for all published articles. Authors may reuse published manuscripts with due acknowledgement. The editor does not accept responsibility for damage or loss of manuscripts or diskettes submitted.

II. Style guide

A. **Quotations** should be double-spaced. Long quotations should also be indented. A copy of the page(s) of the original source of the quotation, as well as a copy of the cover page of that source, should be provided.

B. **Footnotes** should be numbered consecutively throughout the text with Arabic-numeral superscripts. Footnotes should not be used for citing references; these should be placed in the text. Important substantive comments should be integrated in the text itself rather than placed in footnotes.

C. **Figures** (charts, graphs, illustrations, etc.) should have headers, subheaders, labels and full sources. Footnotes to figures should be preceded by lowercase letters and should appear after the sources. Figures should be numbered consecutively. The position of figures in the text should be indicated as follows:

Put figure 1 here

D. **Tables** should have headers, subheaders, column headers and full sources. Table headers should indicate the year(s) of the data, if applicable. The unavailability of data should be indicated by two dots (..). If data are zero or negligible, this should be indicated by a dash (-). Footnotes to tables should be preceded by lower case letters and should appear after the sources. Tables should be numbered consecutively. The position of tables in the text should be indicated as follows:

Put table 1 here

E. **Abbreviations** should be avoided whenever possible, except for FDI (foreign direct investment) and TNCs (transnational corporations).

F. **Bibliographical references** in the text should appear as: "John Dunning (1979) reported that ...", or "This finding has been widely supported in the literature (Cantwell, 1991, p. 19)". The author(s) should ensure that there is a strict correspondence between names and years appearing in the text and those appearing in the list of references.

All citations in the list of references should be complete. Names of journals should not be abbreviated. The following are examples for most citations:

Bhagwati, Jagdish (1988). *Protectionism* (Cambridge, MA: MIT Press).

Cantwell, John (1991). "A survey of theories of international production", in Christos N. Pitelis and Roger Sugden, eds., *The Nature of the Transnational Firm* (London: Routledge), pp. 16-63.

Dunning, John H. (1979). "Explaining changing patterns of international production: in defence of the eclectic theory", *Oxford Bulletin of Economics and Statistics*, 41 (November), pp. 269-295.

United Nations Centre on Transnational Corporations (1991). *World Investment Report 1991: The Triad in Foreign Direct Investment.* Sales No. E.91.II.A.12.

All manuscripts accepted for publication will be edited to ensure conformity with United Nations practice.

READERSHIP SURVEY

Dear Reader,

We believe that *Transnational Corporations,* already in its fourteenth year of publication, has established itself as an important channel for policy-oriented academic research on issues relating to transnational corporations (TNCs) and foreign direct investment (FDI). But we would like to know what **you** think of the journal. To this end, we are carrying out a readership survey. And, as a special incentive, every respondent will receive an UNCTAD publication on TNCs! Please fill in the attached questionnaire and send it to:

> Readership Survey: *Transnational Corporations*
> Karl P. Sauvant
> Editor
> UNCTAD, Room E-10054
> Palais des Nations
> CH-1211 Geneva 10
> Switzerland
> Fax: (41) 22 907 0498
> (E-mail: Karl.Sauvant@UNCTAD.org)

Please do take the time to complete the questionnaire and return it to the above-mentioned address. Your comments are important to us and will help us to improve the quality of *Transnational Corporations*. We look forward to hearing from you.

Sincerely yours,

Karl P. Sauvant
Editor
Transnational Corporations

TRANSNATIONAL CORPORATIONS

Questionnaire

1. Name and address of respondent (optional):

_____

_____

_____

_____

2. In which country are you based?

_____

_____

_____

3. Which of the following best describes your area of work?

Government	☐	Public enterprise	☐
Private enterprise	☐	Academic or research	☐
Non-profit organization	☐	Library	☐
Media	☐	Other (specify)	☐

4. What is your overall assessment of the contents of *Transnational Corporations*?

Excellent	☐	Adequate	☐
Good	☐	Poor	☐

5. How useful is *Transnational Corporations* to your work?

Very useful ☐   Of some use ☐   Irrelevant ☐

6. Please indicate the three things you liked most about *Transnational Corporations*:

_____

_____

_____

7. Please indicate the three things you liked least about *Transnational Corporations*:

    _____

    _____

    _____

    _____

    _____

8. Please suggest areas for improvement:

    _____

    _____

    _____

    _____

    _____

9. Are you a subscriber?   Yes ☐   No ☐

    If not, would you like to become one ($45 per year)? Yes ☐ No ☐
    Please use the subscription form on p. 187).

I wish to subscribe to *Transnational Corporations*

Name   _____

Title   _____

Organization _____

Address   _____

              _____

Country   _____

Subscription rates for *Transnational Corporations* (3 issues per year)

☐ 1 year US$45 (single issue: US$20)

☐ Payment enclosed

Charge my   ☐ Visa   ☐ Master Card   ☐ American Express

Account No. _____ Expiry Date _____

United Nations Publications

Sales Section	Sales Section
Room DC2-853	United Nation Office
2 UN Plaza	Palais des Nations
New York, N.Y. 10017	CH-1211 Geneva 10
United States	Switzerland
Tel: +1 212 963 8302	*Tel*: +41 22 917 2615
Fax: +1 212 963 3484	*Fax*: +41 22 917 0027
E-mail: publications@un.org	*E-mail*: unpubli@unog.ch

Is our mailing information correct?

Let us know of any changes that might affect your receipt of *Transnational Corporations*. Please fill in the new information.

Name   _____

Title   _____

Organization _____

Address   _____

              _____

Country   _____

For further information on UNCTAD's work on investment, technology and enterprise development, please visit:

Division on Investment, Technology and Enterprise Development, DITE
http://www.unctad.org/en/subsites/dite

Transnational Corporations Journal
http://www.unctad.org/tnc

FDI Statistics online
http://www.unctad.org/en/subsites/dite/FDIstats_files/FDIstats.htm

World Investment Report
http://www.unctad.org/wir

Advisory Services on Investment and Training
http://www.unctad.org/asit

International Investment Agreements
http://www.unctad.org/iia

Investment Policy Reviews
http://www.unctad.org/en/investpolicy.en.htm

LDCs Investment Guides
http://www.unctad.org/en/investguide.en.htm

World Association of Investment Promotion Agencies (WAIPA)
http://www.waipa.org

United Nations Conference on Trade and Development, UNCTAD
http://www.unctad.org